MW01680112

SRA

Open Court Reading

Intervention Blackline Masters

Level 2

Program Author
Marsha Roit

SRA
A Division of The McGraw·Hill Companies
Columbus, Ohio

SRA/McGraw-Hill

A Division of The **McGraw-Hill** *Companies*

Send all inquiries to:
SRA/McGraw-Hill
8787 Orion Place
Columbus, OH 43240-4027

Printed in the United States of America.

ISBN 0-02-683925-3

3 4 5 6 7 8 9 VIC 04 03 02 01 00

Table of Contents

Lesson Blackline Masters

Unit 1 Sharing Stories

Unit 2 Kindness

Unit 3 Look Again

Unit 4 Fossils

Unit 5 Courage

Unit 6 Our Country and Its People

Assessment Blackline Masters

Blackline Masters

Name ______________________________ Date __________

BLM 1

Pat had a pet cat, Sam. Sam was Pat's pal. Pat had a pet hen, Sal. Sal was Pat's pal.

Pat's lap held Sam and Sal. Sal had a nap. Sam sat. Sam had a nap. Sal sat. Pat sat and sat and sat. Pat set Sam and Sal on the bed. Pat let Sam and Sal nap.

Pat met Dad and Ted in the den.

"Where are Sam and Sal?"

"Sam and Sal nap and nap and nap on the bed. Sam and Sal plan ten naps a day. I cannot sit for ten naps!"

I read this

silently. ____

aloud. ____

with a partner. ____

with the teacher. ____

Name ______________________ Date __________

BLM 2 Grammar (Common and Proper Nouns)

Read the story and circle the nouns that should begin with a capital letter. Write the noun correctly above each circle. Then write the story correctly on the lines below.

ellen is going to the beach. She is going to see the pacific ocean for the first time. Ellen's friend marie is going with her. Ellen's dog fluffy has to stay home. Grandma made lunch for the trip. The girls will share their stories when they get home on sunday, may 20.

____

____

____

____

____

____

____

____

Name ________________________________ Date ______________

BLM 1

Cam sits in class. Cam looks at books. Cam picks a book. Cam picks *Sam's Cat.* Cam likes *Sam's Cat.* She hands it to her pal Nick.

"Pick *Sam's Cat*, Nick," says Cam. "*Sam's Cat* is a kick."

"OK."

Nick picks *Sam's Cat.* It is a hit! Nick hands it to Ken.

"Pick *Sam's Cat*, Ken," says Nick. "*Sam's Cat* is a kick."

"OK."

Ken picks *Sam's Cat.* It is a hit! Ken hands it to Cam.

"Pick *Sam's Cat*, Cam," says Ken.

"I did!"

I read this

silently. ____

aloud. ____

with a partner. ____

with the teacher. ____

Name ______________________________ Date ______________

BLM 2 Grammar (Subject-Verb Agreement)

Read the story and circle the correct verb for each sentence. Then write each sentence correctly on the lines below.

Kit (get, gets) up in class to tell her story. All the children (sit, sits) around the room. Kit (open, opens) her mouth. They (hear, hears) no sound. Kit's face (turn, turns) red. She (start, starts) to laugh. Then Kit (sit, sits) down.

1. ______________________________
2. ______________________________
3. ______________________________
4. ______________________________
5. ______________________________
6. ______________________________
7. ______________________________

Name ____________________ Date __________

BLM 1

"Get in bed, Max," yelled Mom.

Max had to get his bed fixed. Max got a stack of books. He got a bat. He got six big rocks. He got wax lips. He got his black backpack. He got his best hat. It all went on Max's bed.

Next Max got his soft pets. He got his dog, Rex. He got his cat, Flip. He got his fox, Red. He got his big frog, Hops. He got blankets. It all went on Max's bed.

Mom came in to tuck Max in and tell him a story. Max's bed was packed. Mom had no spot to sit!

I read this

silently. ____

aloud. ____

with a partner. ____

with the teacher. ____

Name ______________________ Date ____________

BLM 2 Grammar (Pronouns and Antecedents)

Read the story and circle the incorrect pronouns. Write the correct pronoun above each circle. Then write the story correctly on the lines below.

Karen's mom likes to read to Karen at bedtime. He curls up on the bed with Karen and Karen's cat, Pete. He reads even if Karen falls asleep. Sometimes our cat is the only one awake. Karen's mom just keeps reading to her. Pete knows a good story when she hears one.

____

____

____

____

____

____

____

____

Name ________________________________ Date ____________

BLM 1

George and Martha Washington had a large farm. George wished to be a farmer. But he had to help win land from the king. He led men in war. Then he went back to his farm.

But he could not farm yet. Men asked him to help plan the land. George had to help. It was a big job. George helped the men and then went back to his farm.

But he could not farm yet. Men asked George to be in charge of the land. Men said that George was smart and strong. Men trusted George. He had to help them. George left his farm and went to run the land. He was the first president.

I read this

silently. ____

aloud. ____

with a partner. ____

with the teacher. ____

Name ____________________ Date __________

BLM 2 Grammar (Proper Nouns)

Read the story and circle the proper nouns that should start with a capital letter. Write the noun correctly above each circle. Then write the story correctly on the lines below.

Mark Twain was a writer. He was one of america's best storytellers. His real name was Samuel clemens. When he was a child, he lived in Hannibal, missouri. He wrote about life on the mississippi River. One of his most famous books is called *tom Sawyer*.

____

____

____

____

____

____

____

____

____

Name ______________________ Date __________

BLM I

The children in Mr. Crane's class had to tell a tale. Each person had to stand facing the class. Most of the class was afraid of making mistakes. Kay felt prepared. She didn't get the jitters. She waited for her turn.

Mr. Crane came up to Kay and faced her. He called her name, and she got up. Kay gazed at the faces in the class. Her legs started to shake. Kay didn't expect this! Her classmates waited for Kay to tell her tale.

Kay took a deep breath and gave the name of her tale. Then she felt brave. Kay told her tale without a mistake. Her classmates were amazed! Mr. Crane praised Kay's good work.

I read this

silently. ____

aloud. ____

with a partner. ____

with the teacher. ____

Name ______________________ Date ____________

BLM 2 Grammar (End Punctuation)

Read the story and circle the incorrect end marks. Write the correct end mark above each circle. Then write the story correctly on the lines below.

Jeff's dad is a writer! He has written about a hundred books? Have you ever read any of them? I have read some of his adventure stories? Jeff's dad travels to interesting places to get ideas! Writing takes a lot of time, but it seems like a great job!

____

____

____

____

____

____

____

____

____

Name ______________________________ Date ______________

BLM 1

Mr. McKenzie makes birdhouses. He spends each day in his shop. He works until long after dark. When he leaves his shop, he is very sleepy. He does not have any energy to clean up.

Mr. McKenzie has secret helpers. When Mr. McKenzie leaves, songbirds sneak into the shop. They clean up for him. They dust and sweep. If you look, you can see the marks of their little feet.

Mr. McKenzie treats the birds to heaps of birdseed. In the tree near his shop, he keeps a sweet, little, green house. He made it just for them. Mr. McKenzie put bells on his kitties. The songbirds can hear the kitties sneak up on them. He doesn't want his kitties to eat his secret helpers!

I read this

silently. ____

aloud. ____

with a partner. ____

with the teacher. ____

Name ______________________ Date ____________

BLM 2 Grammar (Pronouns and Antecedents)

Read the story and circle the incorrect pronouns. Write the correct pronoun above each circle. Then write the story correctly on the lines below.

Pete's dog, Maggie, brings them all kinds of things. She has brought it five bones, three balls, and six shoes. Pete never knows what they will bring home next. But he doesn't really care. She just wants Maggie to be happy. And she is! Maggie knows that Pete will love him no matter what he brings home.

____

____

____

____

____

____

____

____

Name ______________________________ Date ______________

BLM 1

Tyler waited by the driveway. He wanted to see the python that likes to fix bikes. It might slide by! Soon the python glided into sight.

"Hi," said Tyler. "Can you please fix my bike?"

The python looked sly. He was trying to decide on the right price.

"I am delighted to help. Here is my price: you must make me a kite. It must be bright green with white stripes. It must fly to the highest part of the sky."

"That seems all right," said Tyler. "I will be back on Friday with the kite."

"And this bike will be just like brand new," added the python with a smile.

I read this

silently. ____

aloud. ____

with a partner. ____

with the teacher. ____

Name ______________________________ Date ____________

BLM 2 Grammar (Types of Sentences: Capitalization and End Punctuation)

Read the story and circle the incorrect end marks. Also circle words that should begin with a capital letter. Write the correct end mark or capital letter above each circle. Then write each sentence correctly on the lines below.

mrs. Reed met a rabbit in her garden and told it to scat? But do you know what the rabbit did. the rabbit showed her a pile of weeds.

"For three carrots I will weed your garden," he said.

"what a deal." Mrs. Reed thought. now Mrs. Reed's garden is weed free?

1. ______________________________
2. ______________________________
3. ______________________________
4. ______________________________
5. ______________________________
6. ______________________________

Name ______________________________ Date ______________

BLM I

Lois was sad. Her roses did not seem to be growing.

"I know what those roses need," said a troll.

The troll was standing close by. He had on a gold coat and a bow tie.

"Those roses need toast," claimed the troll.

"You must be joking," said Lois.

"No. Roses like toast and yogurt," said the troll.

"If you say so," sighed Lois. She made toast. She put yogurt in a bowl.

"Just leave those things here and go away," said the troll. "These roses will be so happy."

Lois went away. Then the rose ate some yogurt.

"You have to grow, you know. No more snacks for you if you don't grow!" said the troll.

"No problem," said the rose. "Please pass the toast."

I read this

silently. ____

aloud. ____

with a partner. ____

with the teacher. ____

Name ______________________________ Date ____________

BLM 2 Grammar (Verbs: Irregular)

Read the story and circle the incorrect verbs. Write the correct verb above each circle. Then write the story correctly on the lines below.

Last week, I have to clean out my garage. I get a family of squirrels to help me. They swept and mopped every inch. They throw away a stack of junk. They do a lot of work, so I gave them some lemonade and cookies. We make a great team!

Name ____________________ Date ____________

BLM I

Many years ago, there was a queen named Rue. She ruled from the blue sea to the green hills. One day, Queen Rue called her flute player.

"Please play me a tune," begged the queen. "I'm feeling blue."

So the flute player blew Queen Rue a merry tune. Very quickly, Queen Rue felt quite a bit better. The flute player went home.

This happened a few more times. Every time, the flute player's tunes made Queen Rue feel happy.

One day, the flute player got a gift. Queen Rue sent a handmade quilt with blue and yellow squares. Queen Rue sent a brand new silver flute. A note was glued to a blue ribbon tied on the flute. It said "Thank you for your beautiful music. Best wishes from Queen Rue."

I read this

silently.____

aloud. ____

with a partner. ____

with the teacher. ____

Name ______________________________ Date ______________

BLM 2 Grammar (Punctuating Sentences)

Read the story and circle the incorrect end marks. Write the correct end mark above each circle. Then write the story correctly on the lines below.

My friend told me to go see the unicorn at the zoo. He said that the zookeeper found it and put it in a safe place!

"No way!" I said. But I had to go see for myself. I went to the zoo and couldn't believe my eyes? Did you know that unicorns have purple eyes. Well neither did I?

____

____

____

____

____

____

____

____

Name ______________________________________ Date ______________

BLM I

It was late on Tuesday night. Something flew past Julie's window. It was too big to be a hawk. Julie pulled on her boots. She threw on her coat. The moon was shining. The night sky was deep blue.

Julie heard the hoot of an owl. It was in a spruce tree. Julie knew it was a great horned owl. She could see its huge wings.

Julie saw something scoot in the grass. It was Tootsie, her cat. Julie picked up Tootsie. Her fur felt smooth. Her little nose felt cool.

"Thank goodness I got you" whispered Julie. "It is not too safe here for a cute little cat like you!"

I read this

silently. ____

aloud. ____

with a partner. ____

with the teacher. ____

Name ______________________________ Date ______________

BLM 2 Grammar (Pronouns and Antecedents)

Read the story and circle the incorrect pronouns. Write the correct pronoun above each circle. Then write the story correctly on the lines below.

Matt was taking a walk on the beach when she heard something strange. It sounded to them like a crying baby. Then he looked all around and spotted an otter. It had gotten his flipper stuck under a log. Matt couldn't move the log alone, so they got some friends to help him. She rolled the log away and set the otter free.

____

____

____

____

____

____

____

____

Name ______________________ Date ____________

BLM I

Susie has a job feeding pets. In the fall, winter, and spring, Susie's job is easy. She has only her own pets to feed. In summer, Susie is busy. She takes care of pets up and down the street. She feeds pets each and every day. She looks after pets week in and week out.

Susie keeps track of each pet's needs. She knows that Blue likes roast beef. She knows that Pokey likes corn on the cob. She knows that Meany doesn't like crunchy treats. She knows that Daisy likes to have her tummy rubbed.

Hardly anyone takes pets on trips. The pets often stay at home. Luckily, the pets have Susie.

I read this

silently. ____

aloud. ____

with a partner. ____

with the teacher. ____

Name ______________________________ Date ______________

BLM 2 Grammar (Possessive Nouns)

Read the story and circle the words that need an apostrophe. Write the correct word above each circle. Then write the story correctly on the lines below.

Jays summer job is walking dogs. He picks them up at his neighbors houses every day. Then he heads for the park. Jay knows all of the dogs likes and dislikes. Mrs. Changs dog does not like to get his feet wet. Mr. Gordons dog likes to ride in Jays backpack. Lucky likes to chew on Boomers collar when they all stop to rest.

____

____

____

____

____

____

____

____

Name ______________________________ Date ____________

BLM 1

Once upon a time, there was a prince named Andrew. He was strong and smart. But he had one big problem. He couldn't swim. He tried to float. But he dropped like a stone. Every stroke fell with a thud. Once he gulped three quarts of water. Twice he nearly drowned. It was a disaster.

Prince Andrew went to his fairy godmother. She was often not the least bit helpful. But she did try. She swept her wand over Prince Andrew. In a flash he found himself sitting on a raft with a life jacket on. He was floating in the middle of a stream.

"This is terrific!" exclaimed Prince Andrew. He was thrilled! This was better than swimming.

I read this

silently. ____

aloud. ____

with a partner. ____

with the teacher. ____

Name ______________________________ Date ____________

BLM 2 Grammar (Types of Sentences: End Punctuation)

Read the story and circle the incorrect end marks. Write the correct end mark above each circle. Then write the story correctly on the lines below.

Once upon a time, there was a king! He was very unhappy because he could not leave his castle? One day, a bright red bird flew in the king's window and sang a song?

The king smiled and said, "I wish I felt as happy and free as you do."

And do you know what happened. Poof. The king and the bird flew away together?

____

____

____

____

____

____

____

Name ______________________________ Date ______________

BLM 1

Now you see them, now you don't. Just blink. Living things have plenty of tricks to keep them safe.

Many insects seem to vanish when they get near leaves. A walking stick looks like a skinny branch. It has legs like toothpicks. It can sit unseen. When it moves, it looks like a little twig, slipping off a branch.

Moths can blend in with bark and leaves. If they hold still, hungry birds fly right past them.

Speckled shellfish look like rocks. They swim undisturbed in shallow water. Wading birds and sea creatures hunt for something else to swallow.

I read this

silently. ____

aloud. ____

with a partner. ____

with the teacher. ____

Name ________________________________ Date ______________

BLM 2 Grammar (Subject-Verb Agreement in Simple Sentences)

Read the story and circle the incorrect verbs. Write the correct verb above each circle. Then write the story correctly on the lines below.

Ned races over to Dan's house whenever it snows. Dan have a big hill next to his house. It are the best sledding hill around. Children comes from miles away to sled down Dan's hill. Mothers and fathers watches and take pictures. Everyone have a great time!

____

____

____

____

____

____

____

____

____

Name ____________________ Date __________

BLM I

Animals have ways to stay safe. A coat can be just the thing to keep them from being seen if they are running loose. A lion has a smooth, golden coat. It can hide in yellow grass. A kangaroo is a dusty shade. It is not too easy to spot in the bush. A goose can get lost in reeds by a pool. So can a loon.

An animal needs to be in the best coat. A bobcat hunts. Mice hide. If mice can stay hidden, they cannot be eaten so soon. Mice would be doomed in blue coats. Blue mice cannot hide in tan leaves. If a bobcat can hide, it can get a lot to eat. But if a bobcat had a blue coat, it could not hunt. A blue bobcat cannot hide in a tree. A blue bobcat would soon go hungry.

I read this

silently. ____

aloud. ____

with a partner. ____

with the teacher. ____

Name ______________________________ Date ______________

BLM 2 Grammar (Types of Sentences)

Read the story and circle incorrect end marks or add missing end marks. Write the correct end mark above each circle. Then write the story correctly on the lines below.

Some animals have special coloring in the winter. They turn white. They blend in with the snow and ice! You can't even see them! Some wolves and rabbits change from tan or gray to white? A red fox in winter looks as white as this paper? Polar bears stay white all the time! After all, they live in snow all year round!

____

____

____

____

____

____

____

____

____

Name ____________________ Date __________

BLM 1

Sparrow hawks are brown. So are great horned owls. Both can be found scouting for food. They can be seen around twilight. They fly around the edges of woods and crops and streams. But you have to look closely. They may not be easy to spot.

Sparrow hawks and owls fly low. They can float like shadows and fall like leaves. They can gracefully loop over the ground. They can quietly glide over fields, swooping in between rows. They are not loud like crows. They are as soundless as fish in a shallow pond. They don't growl and howl. They don't show to the mice below.

I read this

silently. ____

aloud. ____

with a partner. ____

with the teacher. ____

Name ________________________________ Date ______________

BLM 2 Grammar (Adverbs)

Read the story and choose an adverb from the following list to complete each sentence. Write the word on the line. Then write the story on the lines below.

sharply	deeply	softly
quietly	closely	quickly

The wolf is an interesting animal. The colors of a wolf's fur _______ blend from head to toe. Look _______ to see tan fur turn to brown. Gray fur _______ changes from silver to blue. A wolf looks _______ with eyes that glow like gold. It sniffs _______ with its black nose. Look! There's a wolf watching _______ from behind a tree.

____

____

____

____

____

____

____

Name ______________________________ Date ______________

BLM 1

Mrs. Shaw taught science. She took her class to Cross Creek. They crossed the lawn. They stopped at the gate.

"Watch for paw prints," said Mrs. Shaw. "Keep your eyes open. And take notes! Notes will help you remember everything you see."

The kids started down the path. Dawn caught sight of a fawn. It was standing near the creek. It was not very old. It had spots on its tawny back. It wobbled on its skinny legs as it ran away. It caught up with its mother and disappeared into the woods.

"That was awesome!" said Dawn.

"I'll say," said Mrs. Shaw.

I read this

silently. ____

aloud. ____

with a partner. ____

with the teacher. ____

Name ______________________ Date __________

BLM 2 Grammar (Adverbs and Adjectives)

Read the story. Then circle the adjectives and underline the adverbs. Write each adjective and adverb under the correct head below.

A small, green worm was crawling slowly along a leaf. A big hawk flapped its wings wildly. It landed on a brown log near the leaf. The hawk stared at the leaf with glassy eyes. The tiny worm suddenly stopped and waited. The hawk looked closely. But it did not see the little worm. What luck! The hawk left.

Adjectives	Adverbs
______________	______________
______________	______________
______________	______________
______________	______________
______________	______________
______________	______________
______________	______________

Name ______________________________ Date ____________

BLM I

This is the story of how the platypus got its shape. You will enjoy finding out why it looks so odd.

Once there was an otter. He was a spoiled little fellow. He was noisy and annoying if he didn't get his way.

One day he saw a duck eating moist coils of pond plants. The otter liked the duck's bill. It was a nice color. It seemed handy. The otter decided he had to have a duck bill. He made a big fuss until he got his way.

"There you go," said his mom. "I hope you enjoy it."

A few days later, the otter was trying out his new bill. He was rejoicing at the good choice he had made. Then he saw a beaver. He heard its tail smack the water.

"Oh, boy!" yelled the otter. "I have to have a tail like that!"

I read this

silently. ____

aloud. ____

with a partner. ____

with the teacher. ____

Name ______________________ Date __________

BLM 2 Grammar (Punctuating Dialogue)

Read the story and put an arrow where quotation marks should be. Write quotation marks above each arrow. Then write the story correctly on the lines below.

A bobcat chased a rabbit. The rabbit dove into a pond.

"A little water won't stop me, said the bobcat.

"Look out for your spots!" yelled the rabbit.

The bobcat stopped. He looked surprised.

"What do you mean? asked the bobcat.

You don't want to wash off your spots," said the rabbit. That's why cats don't like water!"

____

____

____

____

____

____

____

Name ______________________________ Date ______________

BLM I

All living things need water. They need it to drink. They drink an awful lot! They cannot get through the day without it. On a hot day, they enjoy a cool dip in a river. You might enjoy it, too!

On a sunny afternoon, all kinds of animals show up on a river bank. You can enjoy watching birds. You can see mammals and their new babies. You can see fish swimming in shallow pools.

The river is peaceful and cool. Sit on a rock and watch the water slowly flow past. Hear the river noises. Hear the howls and hoots and caws of animals that call it home.

I read this

silently. ____

aloud. ____

with a partner. ____

with the teacher. ____

Name ______________________________ Date ____________

BLM 2 Grammar (Nouns)

Read the story and choose a noun from the following list to complete each sentence. Write the noun on the line. Then write each sentence correctly on the lines below.

nest	yard	pond	lawn
deck	goose	Mrs. Chan	crows

Mr. Chan has a __________ in his yard. A __________ from Canada swims there. A flock of __________ hops on the __________. A robin is building a __________ in a hollow tree. __________ put a feeder out on the __________. The Chans have a busy, noisy __________.

1. ______________________________
2. ______________________________
3. ______________________________
4. ______________________________
5. ______________________________
6. ______________________________

Name ______________________ Date ____________

BLM 1

Sand dunes, sea cliffs, and river bluffs are good places to look for fossils. Over time, bones and shells of animals get trapped in the mud and sand. As more mud is plopped and dropped, the bottom layer keeps getting harder. The hard animal remains keep getting buried deeper and deeper.

If you are careful digging down through the layers, you may find pieces of rocks with imprints. It is like putting together a puzzle! And the pieces get older and older the farther down you go.

Some children like to dig in tide pools. They are always digging up something new and exciting. And it is not odd for them to find fossils.

I read this

silently. ____

aloud. ____

with a partner. ____

with the teacher. ____

Name ______________________________ Date ______________

BLM 2 Grammar (Commas in a Series)

Read the story and insert an arrow wherever a comma is needed. Place a comma above each arrow. Then write the story correctly on the lines below.

It is fun to hunt for fossils. They can be found in frozen soil old creek beds and lakes. You might find a fossil of a footprint a fern or a bone. An animal's organs hair and skin disappear quickly. They are not saved over time.

Name ______________________ Date __________

BLM I

Opal has a pet pterodactyl named Lil. When Lil was small, Opal kept her pet in a cage in her room. That worked out just right until Lil got big.

One day Lil flew out of the cage. Lil was flying in a big spiral around Opal's room. Lil knocked over the pencil jar and a metal shelf. Lil made a terrible mess.

Mom said, "That pet is going outside, and that is final!"

And when Mom says it is final, she means now! So Opal's dad made a big purple bird house for Lil. The house is just the right size. Now, Opal has a place to keep Lil. And that makes both Mom and Lil happy.

I read this

silently. ____

aloud. ____

with a partner. ____

with the teacher. ____

Name ______________________________ Date ______________

BLM 2 Grammar (Abbreviations)

Read the story and circle the incorrect abbreviations. Write the correct abbreviation above each circle. Then write the story correctly on the lines below.

Once a year Mtr. Gonzalez goes to the doctor for a checkup. Dtr. Mason has an office downtown on Elm Str. Afterwards, Mr. Gonzalez likes to stop for a snack. He goes to a place called the Snack Shack on Second Av. Then he heads for home on a bus that leaves every Mond. at five.

____

____

____

____

____

____

____

____

____

Name ____________________ Date __________

BLM I

Dinosaurs roamed the earth for hundreds and hundreds of years. Then something happened that caused dinosaurs to disappear. For years, scientists have been trying to get a clear picture of what happened.

Maybe the weather changed. Maybe a volcano blew out dangerous fire, smoke, and ash. Maybe there was a huge earthquake. Maybe a meteor shower hit the earth. Maybe dinosaurs ran out of food and water. No one knows for sure.

Scientists give each notion careful consideration. And little by little, scientists are finding out more about these strange, wondrous creatures. Perhaps in the near future, we will be able to solve the puzzle.

I read this

silently. ____

aloud. ____

with a partner. ____

with the teacher. ____

Name ______________________________ Date ____________

BLM 2 Grammar (Compound Subjects and Predicates)

Read the story and underline the compound subjects. Circle the compound predicates. Then write each compound subject and compound predicate under the correct head.

Heavy rain and snowfall can cause flooding. Lakes and rivers fill up and spill over. The water floods farmland and destroys crops. Sometimes roads and bridges must be closed. Too much water can cause damage and make some places unsafe.

Compound Subjects

____

____

____

Compound Predicates

____

____

____

Name ______________________________ Date ______________

BLM I

Footprints can tell a lot about the animal that made them. Footprints that are huge and deep show that the animal was really big and really heavy. Footprints and a tailprint can show size and shape. Quite possibly, the marks left by claws or nails belong to a meat eater.

Footprints can tell interesting things. If you look closely, you may be able to tell that the animal ran swiftly and lightly on tiptoe. You may be able to see that the animal walked slowly along, flat-footed and clumsy. Footprints left in sand and mud might show a set of webbed toes. Scientists study where footprints came from and where they lead.

I read this

silently. ____

aloud. ____

with a partner. ____

with the teacher. ____

Name ______________________________ Date ______________

BLM 2 Grammar (Subject-Verb Agreement)

Read the story and circle the incorrect verbs. Write the correct verb above each circle. Then write the story correctly on the lines below.

Rabbit tracks is easy to spot in the snow. They are so different from other animal tracks. A rabbit land flat on its back feet. Those tracks is long. A rabbit barely touch its front feet to the ground. The front feet makes small prints. These different prints tells us the rabbit's direction.

____

____

____

____

____

____

____

____

Name ______________________ Date ____________

BLM 1

On a stormy night, Lee had a bad dream. It woke him up. He could see that it was early morning. The sky in the east was an unusal green. The wind was sweeping through the trees.

Suddenly, the wind stopped. Lee had a bad feeling. He leaped out of bed. He looked out the window and spotted a funnel cloud. He started to yell. He screamed for his family to hurry down to the basement for safety. Everyone woke up and went directly for the stairs.

Dad and Mom were really proud of Lee's speedy action in an emergency. The tornado passed by quickly. Thanks to Lee, all was well.

I read this

silently. ____

aloud. ____

with a partner. ____

with the teacher. ____

Name ______________________ Date ____________

BLM 2 Grammar (Letters: Form and Punctuation)

Read the letter and circle the capital letters and punctuation that are missing or incorrect. Write the correct letters or punctuation above each circle. Then write the letter correctly on the lines below.

january 26 2001

dear granny

we're having a great time at the beach? what shells we've collected. They come in so many different shapes and sizes would you like to help us sometime! we would love to have you.

yours truly

Jenny

____

____

____

____

____

____

____

Name ______________________________ Date ______________

BLM I

The knight had been chasing the dragon all day. He finally chased it into a cave. Then he called for his page.

"Stay here and keep watch," the knight said. "I need a snack."

"OK," replied the page.

But the page was shaking with fright. His teeth began to chatter. His knees started shaking. Still he sat and waited for the knight.

"I wonder what is taking the knight so long."

The page sat making plans for his escape if the dragon came out of the cave. But then he heard the dragon snoring and he felt brave!

"If the dragon keeps sleeping," thought the page, "I'll make it until the knight returns."

I read this

silently. ____

aloud. ____

with a partner. ____

with the teacher. ____

Name ______________________________ Date ______________

BLM 2 Grammar (Verbs: Regular and Irregular)

Read the story and circle verbs that are not in the past tense. Write a past tense verb above each circle. Then write the story correctly on the lines below.

A dragon waded into the lake. The water feels so good. But the dragon become stuck in the mud. Soon a knight walks by. The dragon waves for help. Then the knight helps the dragon.

____

____

____

____

____

____

____

____

____

____

Name ______________________________ Date ____________

BLM I

An old tale passed down for centuries tells how sunshine came to the world. Long ago, when all skies were dark, a black raven turned himself into a baby. His mother loved him and cared for him, while he waited to trick her! He wanted the sunlight that his grandfather kept hidden inside a box. That box hid inside a bigger box. And that box hid inside a bigger box!

The baby fussed and kicked until his mother showed him the boxes that held the sunlight. Finally, she opened them all. She showed her baby the sunlight. The baby grabbed a piece of sunbeam and held on tight. Then he turned back into a bird. He held the sunbeam in his beak and flew up high into the sky. And the world was flooded with light.

I read this

silently. ____

aloud. ____

with a partner. ____

with the teacher. ____

Name ______________________________ Date ______________

BLM 2 Grammar (Possessive Nouns)

Read the story and circle the possessive nouns are not correct. Write the word correctly above each circle. Then write the story correctly on the lines below.

Kens' career began in Jan's workshop. Jan ran her dads' wood shop with three carpenters. The carpenter's job was to build boats. Many other worker's skills were needed to make fine sailboats. Ken soon became Jans' best carpenter.

____

____

____

____

____

____

____

____

____

Name ______________________ Date ____________

BLM I

After a long, hard day, an African-American woman named Rosa Parks got on a city bus in Montgomery, Alabama. A white man got on after her. He wanted her seat. Rosa Parks did not want to give up her seat. The man told her to get up. She wouldn't get up. The bus driver told her to get up. She wouldn't get up. Rosa Parks was tired. She was tired of following unfair rules.

The bus driver called the police, and Rosa Parks was arrested. Her actions that day led Dr. Martin Luther King, Jr., to start a boycott of all city buses. For 381 days, people who believed in fairness and equal rights for every person used feet, bikes, and cars instead of city buses. The actions of Rosa Parks on that December day made her an American hero.

I read this

silently. ____

aloud. ____

with a partner. ____

with the teacher. ____

Name ______________________ Date ____________

BLM 2 Grammar (Letters: Form and Punctuation)

Read the letter and circle the capital letters and punctuation that are missing or incorrect. Write the correct letters or punctuation above each circle. Then write the letter correctly on the lines below.

june 12 2001

Dear Mark,

we are in Washington, D.C. visiting the Capital Building. Today, I met the senator from my state? He used to work with my dad what a nice man he is.

I can't wait to tell you all about our trip!

your friend

Carly

____

____

____

____

____

____

____

Name ________________________________ Date ____________

BLM I

Farmer Kasper had a chicken, a rooster, and a hamster. The hamster chattered and played all night long. It kept the chicken and the rooster awake. When morning came, the rooster couldn't keep his eyes open. He didn't see the sun come up. He didn't wake up Farmer Kasper and his wife.

Then Farmer Kasper had an idea! He taught the hamster to ring a bell at the crack of dawn.

Now, at the crack of dawn the hamster rings a bell to wake up Farmer Kasper. Then the hamster falls asleep. The chicken cackles and lays an egg for Farmer Kasper. Then she falls asleep. And the silly old rooster just sleeps through the whole thing.

I read this

silently. ____

aloud. ____

with a partner. ____

with the teacher. ____

Name ______________________________ Date ______________

BLM 2 Grammar (Commas in a Series)

Read the story and insert an arrow wherever a comma is needed. Place a comma above each arrow. Then write the story correctly on the lines below.

One day a little girl showed her mother a penny a nickel and a quarter.

"I was with Grandpa," said the little girl. "He gave me a penny for my thoughts. But I told him that they were worth more than a penny. So he smiled laughed and gave me a nickel. Then I told him that I was thinking wishing and hoping for a shiny quarter."

____

____

____

____

____

____

____

Name ______________________________ Date ____________

BLM I

James worked at a wildlife refuge for wolves. It was a large fenced place on the edge of the state forest. Inside the fence, wolf pups were closely studied as they grew from helpless newborn babies into big and strong adults. Outside the fence, many dangers might threaten these little pups. It was James's job to protect them.

When the wolves got older and grew bigger, James knew that he had to let them go. First he loaded them into cages. Later, while the wolves slept, James and his crew took them to their new home in the wild. They would wake up in this new place, ready to explore. James was sad to say good-bye to the wolves he knew and loved so well. But he was happy that the wolves were free.

I read this

silently. ____

aloud. ____

with a partner. ____

with the teacher. ____

Name ______________________ Date ____________

BLM 2 Grammar (Review Parts of Speech: Nouns, Adjectives, and Adverbs)

Read the story and underline the nouns, circle the adjectives, and draw a box around the adverbs. Then write each noun, adjective, and adverb under the correct head.

A young mother closely watched her playful child. The curious child crept slowly toward a tall bookcase. He gently touched a large book. The happy child sat quietly and turned the colorful pages.

Noun	Adjective	Adverb
______	______	______
______	______	______
______	______	______
______	______	______
______	______	______
______	______	______
______	______	______

Name ______________________________ Date ______________

BLM I

People have always had different reasons for traveling to the United States and starting new lives. Leaving behind home and family is very hard. Even when they are glad to be here, people can still feel uprooted and lost. They miss old ways and old friends left behind. They may be unsure about the future and their new lives.

But everybody settling in the United States is looking for freedom and a chance at a better life. People will give up everything to find that. All people coming here bring one thing with them. They bring hope.

I read this

silently. ____

aloud. ____

with a partner. ____

with the teacher. ____

Name ______________________ Date ____________

BLM 2 Grammar (Abbreviations)

Read the story and circle the incorrect abbreviations. Write the correct abbreviation above each circle. Then write the story on the lines below.

Michael delivers newspapers to people in his neighborhood. Every Sund. he takes a paper to Dtr. Sharma and Msr. Boyle on Oak Str. Every Fry. he takes a paper to Mtr. Graham on Beech Av. In Sept., Michael will have delivered papers for three years.

____

____

____

____

____

____

____

____

____

Name ______________________________ Date ______________

BLM I

When my family came to the city, we didn't know anyone at all. It was scary! Everything was so big and noisy. It was hard to feel at home. I missed a lot of things about the farm.

I sent long letters back home to Grandma, telling her all about the new sights and smells. We lived over a bakery. Every morning, the toasty smell floating up through the windows would wake me up. I told Grandma that I had a big soft bed, just as nice as a warm loaf of bread! I begged Grandma to tell me all the news about home.

And then one day, I looked out my window at the rooftops and listened to the busy world outside. I realized I felt right at home just where I was!

I read this

silently. ____

aloud. ____

with a partner. ____

with the teacher. ____

Name ______________________ Date ____________

BLM 2 Grammar (Verbs: Regular and Irregular)

Read the story and circle the incorrect verbs. Write the correct past-tense verb above each circle. Then write the story correctly on the lines below.

Every day after school, Jack walkt his dog, Nikki. It was a chore. Nikki taked her time and smelled everything along the way.

Then one day Jack thinked of a plan. He decide to take along another dog to make the walks more fun. The idea workt well. Nikki gotten more exercise. They all have more fun.

____

____

____

____

____

____

____

____

Name ____________________ Date __________

BLM I

When Thomas Jefferson sat down to write the Declaration of Independence, he didn't really know yet what he was going to say or how he was going to say it. But he did know two things. He knew what he thought was right. He knew what he thought was wrong. That seemed like a good place for him to start.

Jefferson also knew that he had to make room for lots of different thoughts and beliefs.

"We need to be able to disagree without fighting," Jefferson declared. "And we need to be able to have different opinions without being fearful."

Jefferson wrestled his thoughts down on paper. Now in our time, we are living out his dream of freedom.

I read this

silently. ____

aloud. ____

with a partner. ____

with the teacher. ____

Name ______________________________ Date ______________

BLM 2 Grammar (Commas in a Series)

Read the story and insert an arrow wherever a comma is needed. Place a comma above each arrow. Then write the sentences on the lines below.

Once a month, Moira goes into the city with her grandmother. She loves seeing all the traffic the people and the tall buildings. They ride a taxi past Third, Fourth, and Fifth Avenues. Then they stop at a large department store. Moira's grandmother wants to buy a dress a pair of shoes and a purse. Moira soon gets tired. She can't wait to get back in the car drive home and go to bed.

____

____

____

____

____

____

____

Name ______________________________ Date ______________

BLM I

Of all the women that visitors meet in the United States, they most likely remember this one best. She is very tall, and she is very strong. She holds up a light showing the way. She is the Statue of Liberty.

She greets everybody entering New York City. Whether you just came in from a faraway land or you're a returning traveler, this lady stands ready to greet you. She gives hope to all men, women, and children seeking a new life. She looks out for those returning home.

I read this

silently. ____

aloud. ____

with a partner. ____

with the teacher. ____

Name ______________________ Date ____________

BLM 2 Grammar (Compound Sentences)

Read the story and underline the compound sentences. Then write each compound sentence on the lines below.

The Statue of Liberty stands 152 feet high, and it weighs 225 tons. Many people see her, and they can't believe her size. She carries a torch in her right hand, and she holds a tablet in her left. She was a gift from the French government. Years ago, the French and Americans placed her in New York Harbor.

Compound Sentences

____

____

____

____

____

____

____

____

Name ______________________________ Date ______________

BLM I

When we were first starting out on our trip west, Mama couldn't stop crying. Leaving all her family and friends was so hard. We walked far before she would talk to us at all.

In the evening, Daddy wanted to cheer Mama up. He took out his fiddle. Mama always said it sounded like chalk on a slate. I thought it sounded like the cat that had caught a cold.

"I thought you left that awful thing back at the farm!" teased Mama, holding her ears.

"No," said Daddy. "I am going to play it every night. By the time we get to Oregon, I ought to be good!"

I read this

silently. ____

aloud. ____

with a partner. ____

with the teacher. ____

Name ______________________ Date __________

BLM 2 Grammar (Subject-Verb Agreement)

Read the story and circle the incorrect verbs. Write the correct verb above each circle. Then write the story correctly on the lines below.

My family and I walks a long way to California. The days and weeks on the trail is long and hard. Sometimes it are very dry. We chokes and coughs on the clouds of dust. It rain and snow on our trip. Then the road are muddy. At times, the horses could hardly walk.

____

____

____

____

____

____

____

____

Name ______________________________ Date ______________

BLM I

I never thought that I would come back to Gran's cottage. We moved so far away, and it was so hard to get there, it seemed like we would never make such a trip again. But here we are! Gran is so tickled to see us. It seems like we've been gone only a week instead of a whole year.

Things here have scarcely changed. In fact, Gran declared that I am the only thing that is different. That is because I've grown like a weed. My ankles stick out of my socks, and it takes them a long time to reach the cuff of my pants!

Gran said she will make me a new pair before I go home again, and maybe a jacket, too. I can't wait!

I read this

silently. ____

aloud. ____

with a partner. ____

with the teacher. ____

Name ______________________________ Date ______________

BLM 2 Grammar (Abbreviations)

Read the story and circle the incorrect abbreviations. Write the correct abbreviation above each circle. Then write the story correctly on the lines below.

Last week, I went to see my doctor on Clark Sts. Drr. Carter couldn't believe how tall I was. Neither could his nurse, Msr. King. The chart said that in Octo. I was 49 inches tall. In Feb I was 52 inches tall. Now I am taller than all the kids on Baker Ave.

____

____

____

____

____

____

____

____

____

Name ____________________ Date ____________

BLM I

When we left home, we had to leave quickly in the middle of the night. There was hardly time to pack a bag. We had known that the river may flood and we were ready to go. Still it didn't seem real.

I was afraid that I would have to leave my kitten behind. I carefully tucked her inside the pocket of my raincoat. I told her to be very quiet and still until we were safe on the airplane.

Raindrops plopped on the windshield as we drove to the airport. We climbed into Uncle Will's plane. It was hardly bigger than our car. We put on our seatbelts. As we sped down the runway, Mom took my hand.

"You didn't forget Stripe, did you?" she asked.

"Forget Stripe?" I said, patting my pocket. "No way!"

I read this

silently. ____

aloud. ____

with a partner. ____

with the teacher. ____

Name ______________________________ Date ______________

BLM 2 Grammar (Possessive Nouns)

Read the story and circle the incorrect possessive nouns. Write the correct word above each circle. Then write the story correctly on the lines below.

Uncle Wills airplane is really small. It is like flying around in the Reeds van. Flying in his plane made my only brothers stomach feel sick. But I do not mind the bumps, and I think the planes' seats are cozy. I like to look down at people's houses. It is fun to wonder about each families' life.

____

____

____

____

____

____

____

____

____

Name ______________________________ Date ____________

BLM I

Everybody in Wayne's family is coming to stay for the holidays. They are arriving from all over the United States. Uncle Leo is coming all the way from Maine. It will be an amazing trick to fit such a big group in such a little space. Wayne's mom has been cooking for days. Wayne's dad painted the dining room. It used to be dark blue. Now it is light blue. Wayne's mom likes it. Wayne's dad hates it. But nobody has time to do it again.

When everybody gets here, the party will be noisy and cheerful. Everybody will be speaking at once. Everybody will eat and sing and have a happy time. No one will notice the blue of the dining room. After everybody leaves, Wayne's dad can get out his paintbrush. Wayne thinks that a nice, rosy pink would be neat!

I read this

silently. ____

aloud. ____

with a partner. ____

with the teacher. ____

Name ______________________________ Date ______________

BLM 2 Grammar (Letters: Form and Punctuation)

Read the letter and circle incorrect or missing capitalization and punctuation. Write the correct capitalization or punctuation above each circle. Then write the letter correctly on the lines below.

may 12 2001

dear aunt Anne

Thank you for the interesting book. You always know the best books to read? It was fun learning about the life of a skater. Now I want to practice even harder

sincerely!

Grace.

____

____

____

____

____

____

____

Assessment

Introduction

The assessment component of the ***Intervention Guide*** is intended to be administered to students with the support of a teacher or teacher aide. The assessments focus on a number of aspects of reading: oral fluency for reading both words and continuous prose, comprehension, vocabulary, and related language arts skills. The ***Intervention*** assessment is intended to serve several purposes:

- ✔ review students' recall of what they were taught in an ***Intervention*** unit
- ✔ measure students' ability to apply a broad range of general reading skills
- ✔ determine areas of relative strength and weakness in students' reading ability

Before proceeding further, it is important to emphasize that the students for whom the ***Intervention Guide*** is appropriate do not read as well as their peers. They are probably experiencing some frustration when it comes to reading and to school as well, so their tolerance for challenge may be low. Given these circumstances, it is important that you, the teacher, should feel free to exercise your professional judgment in administering the assessments. If you believe that modifying an assessment will make it more appropriate for your students, you should undertake the modification.

Before administering the assessments, be sure the students understand that they will not be graded on their performance. Let them know that they should do their best, and that any mistakes they make will help you teach them better. The more relaxed and confident students feel while completing the assessments, the more likely it is that their performance will reflect their true abilities. In fact, by establishing a non-threatening environment for the assessment, you will find that students are more likely to take risks and thus improve their attitude toward reading while they improve their skills.

Oral Word Reading Assessment

The first assessment is an oral word reading task. Students simply read a series of words while you record their performance. For the most part, the words feature the letters and sounds found in a unit or those that were taught previously. Some of the words, however, will unavoidably contain a sound that might be new to students, particularly in the assessment for Unit 1. For example, the word *phone* may be included in the word reading assessment because it is the most familiar word that uses the *ph* sound. Unfortunately, the Long o sound may not be introduced until later, so students may stumble over it. When you evaluate students' performance on the oral word reading assessment, you should keep this limitation in mind and focus on the skills to which the student has been exposed.

Ideally, students should read all of the words on the list because it will provide you with the most accurate estimate of their ability. If students are making frequent errors or seem frustrated, it will be helpful to have them read just one or two lines of words, take a short break, and then continue. It is better to spend a little more time on the assessment and get useful information than to hurry through it, frustrate the student, and gain little understanding of a student's ability. If students are exceedingly frustrated, however, it is best to terminate the assessment.

Oral Fluency Assessment

The most important source of information about the skill level of poor readers is an oral fluency assessment. By listening to students read continuous prose out loud, you will receive invaluable information about students' abilities in a broad range of skills, from simple decoding to cadence, joining related words in phrases, and comprehending while reading.

As was true with the oral word reading assessment, it is more useful to have students attempt the entire passage. If the students become too frustrated, however, simply stop the assessment. **Students who cannot read the oral fluency assessment independently, including self-corrections, should not be expected to complete the remaining assessments independently.**

The oral fluency assessment includes a majority of words that are decodable or are high-frequency words with which students are probably familiar. There are some words, however, that contain phonetic elements that students might not yet have been taught. As was true with the oral word reading assessment, you should focus your evaluation primarily on sounds that the students have been taught. As a secondary evaluation, you may note students' ability to deal with novel sounds.

Comprehension Assessment

If students have demonstrated the ability to read the oral fluency passage successfully, they should be given an opportunity to read the comprehension passage silently and answer the questions on their own. If students are unable to read the oral fluency passage successfully, it is unlikely that they will be able to read the comprehension passage independently, so you should consider the following alternatives:

1. For students who are reading somewhat below grade level, read the passage aloud with the student, prompting the student when necessary. If the student appears able to read sections on his or her own, allow them to do so. When they come to stumbling points, begin reading along with the student and prompting again. Continue the process with the comprehension questions that follow the passage, reading along with the students as necessary, but allow the student to choose the answers independently.
2. For students who are reading significantly below grade level, read the comprehension passage out loud while the student follows along silently. While you read, ask brief questions periodically to prompt the student's understanding of the passage. When you have finished reading the passage, read the questions and see if the student can answer them independently. If necessary, reread portions of the passage and then read the question again. This process will encourage students and help them become familiar with the process of comprehension assessment.

Vocabulary and Skills Assessments

The vocabulary and skills assessment sections contain a variety of items covering the skills featured in a unit. We recommend that a teacher or teacher aide be available to read the directions in bold to the student. Moreover, only students who can read the fluency assessment passage independently should complete the vocabulary and skills assessments on their own.

For students who need the help completing the vocabulary and skills assessments, you should follow procedures similar to those outlined above for the comprehension assessment: read the items along with the students who are somewhat below grade level, and read the items to students who are significantly below grade level. Encourage students to participate in the assessment to the best of their ability, and use the assessment process to determine how well the students understand the underlying skills that are featured in each item.

A Final Word

For many students, particularly students who are having difficulty learning to read, assessment of any kind can be an unpleasant experience. However, this need not be the case. Assessment can be a positive learning experience. Through assessment, the teacher can gain valuable insights into the students' abilities and give extra assistance where needed. Providing such assistance to students will build a bond between the teacher and students, diminish the stigma students feel about not reading as well as their peers, and instill in them the confidence they need to become independent readers.

Oral Word Reading Assessment

1	sat	bed	him	log	fun
2	same	pay	wait	came	king
3	knock	her	dirt	turn	thin
4	both	write	phone	chair	match
5	page	gate	edge	jar	wish
6	white	wave	wax	city	race
7	yell	giant	buzz	this	bird

Student Record: Oral Word Reading Assessment

Name ______________________________ **Date** ______________

1	sat	bed	him	log	fun
2	same	pay	wait	came	king
3	knock	her	dirt	turn	thin
4	both	write	phone	chair	match
5	page	gate	edge	jar	wish
6	white	wave	wax	city	race
7	yell	giant	buzz	this	bird

Directions: Have the students read each word slowly. They should begin at the top-left and move from left to right, sweeping back to the beginning of the next row of words after finishing the last word in a row. You may stop the assessment if you sense that the student is becoming frustrated or if the student fails to read three consecutive words correctly.

Scoring: Draw a line through each word that the student reads incorrectly. If possible, circle or underline the letters that are the source of the error. It will be helpful to phonetically write the mispronunciation for any incorrect word. This information may be useful in identifying the areas in which a student needs additional instruction or practice. In the space below, write the number of words the student attempted and the number read correctly.

Words Attempted: ______ **Words Correct:** ______ **Percent Correct:** ______

Oral Fluency Assessment

Nick is a big, brown dog. He has a black nose and funny ears. Nick likes to play catch. When you throw the ball, he will run after it. Then he will bring it back to you. He sits down in front of you and wags his tail. He holds the ball in his mouth. When Nick wants to play, this is what he does. He gets his ball. Then he walks up to you. He drops his ball at your feet. He looks at you until you throw the ball for him. If you throw it, you will make him happy.

Student Record: Oral Fluency Assessment

Name ______________________________ **Date** ______________

Nick is a big, brown dog. He has a black nose and funny ears. Nick likes to play catch. When you throw the ball, he will run after it. Then he will bring it back to you. He sits down in front of you and wags his tail. He holds the ball in his mouth. When Nick wants to play, this is what he does. He gets his ball. Then he walks up to you. He drops his ball at your feet. He looks at you until you throw the ball for him. If you throw it, you will make him happy.

	Error Count	Error Total
Inserting an extra word	______________	(______)
Omitting a word	______________	(______)
Substituting words	______________	(______)
Refusing to attempt a word	______________	(______)
Mispronouncing a word	______________	(______)
Repeating a word	______________	(______)
Reversing words	______________	(______)
(0-3 errors=independent; 4-6 errors=instructional; 7+errors=frustration)	**Total:**	**(______)**

What is your estimation of this student's ability to read this text with fluency, accuracy, pacing, intonation, expression, and understanding? Circle the number that best reflects your estimation.

Below Average for this grade		Average for this grade		Above Average for this grade
1	2	3	4	5

Comprehension Assessment

"What do you think, Alan?" asked Mother.

"It's perfect, Mom," answered Alan. "It's the best bike ever. I can't wait to ride it."

"Before you ride it, let's talk about safety. You must always wear a helmet. You must ride on the sidewalk. And you must tell me or your father where you are going." Mother handed a helmet to Alan as she spoke.

"I'll do all those things, Mom," said Alan. "That's a neat helmet. I'll always wear it, I promise. Can I ride over to Beth's house?"

"Yes," said mother. "That's a good place to ride. Your cousin will be happy to see you. Call as soon as you get there. I will call Aunt Lisa and Uncle Pat now. I will tell them you are coming over."

Alan put on his helmet. He waved at his mother. Then he got on his new bike. He rode down the street with a big smile on his face.

Name ______________________ Date ____________

Comprehension Assessment

1. This story is mostly about
- ◯ a boy who gets a bike
- ◯ a boy and his mother
- ◯ riding a bike

2. Which of these is most important to Alan's mother?
- ◯ riding very far
- ◯ riding fast
- ◯ riding safely

3. Where will Alan ride first?
- ◯ to his friend's house
- ◯ to his cousin's house
- ◯ to school with a friend

4. Before he started riding, what did Alan do first?
- ◯ looked at his tires
- ◯ waved to his mother
- ◯ put on his helmet

5. When Alan gets to his cousin's house, he will
- ◯ call home
- ◯ ride some more
- ◯ eat a snack

Name ______________________ Date __________

Vocabulary Assessment

Read the sentences. Draw a line under each compound word.

1. The cat saw something. It looked out the window. Then it ran through the doorway into the bedroom.

Read the sentences and look at the underlined word. Fill in the space beside the answer that means the opposite of the underlined word.

2. The floor of my room is very clean.
   - ○ large
   - ○ dirty
   - ○ flat

3. All the children were very quiet.
   - ○ loud
   - ○ good
   - ○ happy

4. I read a funny story last night.
   - ○ long
   - ○ strange
   - ○ sad

Read the sentences. Fill in the spaces beside the correct contraction that means the same thing as the underlined words.

5. This is not my coat.
   - ○ isnt
   - ○ is'nt
   - ○ isn't

6. Annie did not call me.
   - ○ didn't
   - ○ did'nt
   - ○ didnt

7. My friends are not ready yet.
   - ○ arent
   - ○ aren't
   - ○ are'nt

8. We will have a snack.
   - ○ well
   - ○ we'll
   - ○ w'ell

Name ______________________ Date ____________

Skills Assessment

Read the sentences. Draw a line under each common noun. Draw a circle around each proper noun.

1. It was a warm day in July. The children swam in the cool water of Lake Waldo. Mary rowed her boat near the shore.

Read the sentences. Draw a line under each verb.

2. Kim walked quickly down the street. She saw her friend, Stan. He said hello to Kim. They talked for a little bit.

Read the sentences. Draw a line under the pronoun in each sentence. Draw a circle around the noun to which it refers.

3. Sam was tired because he had worked hard.

4. The house was small, but it was very nice.

5. Ask Linda and Chet if they want to play a board game.

Read the sentences. Draw a line under each adjective.

6. Put the new table beside the brown chair. We can put a small lamp on the table.

Read the sentences. Put the right punctuation mark at the end of each sentence.

7. That is a good story

8. Did you eat lunch yet

9. Watch out for that bee

10. How old are you

Oral Word Reading Assessment

1	bring	cry	he	see	few
2	very	these	hear	field	nose
3	flag	glad	child	tie	true
4	time	fly	high	quick	use
5	cold	most	home	toe	usual
6	boat	know	truth	blue	show
7	rule	chew	food	barn	cart

Student Record: Oral Word Reading Assessment

Name ______________________________ **Date** ______________

1	bring	cry	he	see	few
2	very	these	hear	field	nose
3	flag	glad	child	tie	true
4	time	fly	high	quick	use
5	cold	most	home	toe	usual
6	boat	know	truth	blue	show
7	rule	chew	food	barn	cart

Directions: Have the students read each word slowly. They should begin at the top-left and move from left to right, sweeping back to the beginning of the next row of words after finishing the last word in a row. You may stop the assessment if you sense that the student is becoming frustrated or if the student fails to read three consecutive words correctly.

Scoring: Draw a line through each word that the student reads incorrectly. If possible, circle or underline the letters that are the source of the error. It will be helpful to phonetically write the mispronunciation for any incorrect word. This information may be useful in identifying the areas in which a student needs additional instruction or practice. In the space below, write the number of words the student attempted and the number read correctly.

Words Attempted: ______ **Words Correct:** ______ **Percent Correct:** ______

Oral Fluency Assessment

Dan was sad. He had lost his best hat. It was a gift from his father. Dan did not know where to look. He had been with his friends. They had been playing. Dan's friends did not know what to do to help. They wanted to make him happy. His friends tried to think of something to do. Then Carol came running up. She had found Dan's hat! It was on the ground near the school. Now Dan was happy. He said thank you to Carol. She said you are welcome. He had the hat he liked most of all.

Student Record: Oral Fluency Assessment

Name ______________________________ Date ______________

Dan was sad. He had lost his best hat. It was a gift from his father. Dan did not know where to look. He had been with his friends. They had been playing. Dan's friends did not know what to do to help. They wanted to make him happy. His friends tried to think of something to do. Then Carol came running up. She had found Dan's hat! It was on the ground near the school. Now Dan was happy. He said thank you to Carol. She said you are welcome. He had the hat he liked most of all.

	Error Count	Error Total
Inserting an extra word	______________	(_____)
Omitting a word	______________	(_____)
Substituting words	______________	(_____)
Refusing to attempt a word	______________	(_____)
Mispronouncing a word	______________	(_____)
Repeating a word	______________	(_____)
Reversing words	______________	(_____)
(0-3 errors=independent; 4-6 errors=instructional; 7+errors=frustration)	**Total:**	**(_____)**

What is your estimation of this student's ability to read this text with fluency, accuracy, pacing, intonation, expression, and understanding? Circle the number that best reflects your estimation.

Below Average for this grade		Average for this grade		Above Average for this grade
1	2	3	4	5

Comprehension Assessment

Every day, Jenny stopped by Mrs. King's house. She helped Mrs. King. Sometimes Jenny cut the grass. Sometimes she went to the store. She always helped out.

Brad was Jenny's friend. He asked why she helped Mrs. King.

Jenny said, "It makes me feel good."

Brad thought about this. He went with her one day. Jenny and Brad raked leaves. When they were done, Mrs. King had a snack for them. She showed them pictures. They were from long ago. Mrs. King knew Brad's grandmother. They were friends long ago.

Brad and Jenny walked home.

Brad said, "Jenny, you were right. Helping Mrs. King made me feel good."

Jenny added, "Do you know what else? Because you helped, it was more fun than ever. I hope you will come with me to visit Mrs. King again."

Name ______________________ Date ____________

Comprehension Assessment

1. This story is mostly about children
- ○ playing sports
- ○ in school
- ○ helping

2. Which of these does Jenny do for Mrs. King?
- ○ mow the lawn
- ○ read a book
- ○ wash a car

3. After they raked leaves, Brad and Jenny
- ○ went swimming
- ○ had a snack
- ○ watched a video

4. A good title for this story is
- ○ "A Job"
- ○ "Playing"
- ○ "Helping"

5. Who does Mrs. King know?
- ○ Jenny's mother
- ○ Brad's grandmother
- ○ the teacher in school

Name ______________________ Date __________

Vocabulary Assessment

Read the sentences. Fill in the space beside the adjective that fits best in the blank.

1. Who caught the ____________ fish, you, Tom, or Donna?
   ○ big ○ biggest ○ bigger

2. It is ____________ today than yesterday.
   ○ colder ○ cold ○ coldest

3. We stopped playing because it was ____________.
   ○ darkest ○ darker ○ dark

Read the sentences. Draw a line under each <u>time or order</u> <u>word.</u>

4. The first thing the campers did was put the tent up. Then they started a fire. After that, they cooked their supper. Finally, they went to sleep.

Read the sentences. In the blank, write the plural form of the word in parentheses.

5. There were too many (fly) __flies__ at the picnic.

6. My dog had five (puppy) __puppies__.

7. The tree had more (cherry) __cherries__ than last year.

Read the sentences. Fill in the space beside the word that means the <u>same</u> as the underlined word.

8. The duck swam <u>below</u> the water.
   ○ around ○ above ○ under

9. A loud <u>noise</u> made us jump.
   ○ sound ○ light ○ song

10. Don't trip on that big <u>rock</u>.
    ○ log ○ stone ○ rope

Name ______________________ Date ____________

Skills Assessment

Read the sentences. Fill in the space beside the verb that is spelled right and fits in the blank.

1. The phone __________ a few minutes ago.
   ○ ring ○ rang ○ ringed

2. Dad __________ his car keys, but found them.
   ○ lost ○ lose ○ losed

3. Dana __________ the ball to Steve.
   ○ throwed ○ throw ○ threw

Read the sentences. Draw a line under the pronoun in each sentence. Draw a circle around the noun to which it refers.

4. My sister hurt her knee playing soccer.
5. Laura and Matt want Bud to call them.
6. Carol, can you help set the table?
7. The cat played with its ball.

Read the sentences. In the blank, write the possessive form of the word in parentheses.

8. One of the (car) ______________ tires is flat.
9. That is (Judy) ______________ pen.
10. My uncle showed us an (owl) ______________ nest.
11. This restaurant is (Chicago) ______________ finest.
12. Give me all the (boys) ______________ hats.

Oral Word Reading Assessment

1	spring	noise	grow	clock	string
2	good	write	snow	those	swim
3	trip	front	call	soon	woof
4	each	play	quick	arm	how
5	screen	out	black	spend	watch
6	skunk	talk	slip	toy	saw
7	knot	because	start	kept	shell

Student Record: Oral Word Reading Assessment

Name ______________________________ **Date** ____________

1	spring	noise	grow	clock	string
2	good	write	snow	those	swim
3	trip	front	call	soon	woof
4	each	play	quick	arm	how
5	screen	out	black	spend	watch
6	skunk	talk	slip	toy	saw
7	knot	because	start	kept	shell

Directions: Have the students read each word slowly. They should begin at the top-left and move from left to right, sweeping back to the beginning of the next row of words after finishing the last word in a row. You may stop the assessment if you sense that the student is becoming frustrated or if the student fails to read three consecutive words correctly.

Scoring: Draw a line through each word that the student reads incorrectly. If possible, circle or underline the letters that are the source of the error. It will be helpful to phonetically write the mispronunciation for any incorrect word. This information may be useful in identifying the areas in which a student needs additional instruction or practice. In the space below, write the number of words the student attempted and the number read correctly.

Words Attempted: ______ **Words Correct:** ______ **Percent Correct:** ______

Oral Fluency Assessment

Bugs come in all shapes and colors. Some are big and some are small. Some are very strange. The "walking stick" is one of these strange bugs. It looks just like a small stick. It has a very thin body. It is brown and gray, almost the same color as wood. It has six thin legs. The only way you know it is alive is when it walks. When people see a walking stick, they are surprised. They think they are looking at a stick. Then it starts to walk away. Only when you look closely can you tell it is a bug, not a stick.

Student Record: Oral Fluency Assessment

Name ______________________________ **Date** ______________

Bugs come in all shapes and colors. Some are big and some are small. Some are very strange. The "walking stick" is one of these strange bugs. It looks just like a small stick. It has a very thin body. It is brown and gray, almost the same color as wood. It has six thin legs. The only way you know it is alive is when it walks. When people see a walking stick, they are surprised. They think they are looking at a stick. Then it starts to walk away. Only when you look closely can you tell it is a bug, not a stick.

	Error Count	Error Total
Inserting an extra word	______________	(_____)
Omitting a word	______________	(_____)
Substituting words	______________	(_____)
Refusing to attempt a word	______________	(_____)
Mispronouncing a word	______________	(_____)
Repeating a word	______________	(_____)
Reversing words	______________	(_____)

(0-3 errors=independent; 4-6 errors=instructional; 7+errors=frustration) **Total: (_____)**

What is your estimation of this student's ability to read this text with fluency, accuracy, pacing, intonation, expression, and understanding? Circle the number that best reflects your estimation.

Below Average for this grade		Average for this grade		Above Average for this grade
1	2	3	4	5

Comprehension Assessment

Tigers are big cats. They live in India. A tiger's coat has two colors. A tiger is mostly brownish orange. It has black stripes.

In the zoo, a tiger is easy to see. Its colors are bright. In the jungle, a tiger is hard to see. A tiger looks like the other things in the jungle. Other animals cannot see the tiger. It hunts them. A tiger can get close to the animals it hunts.

A zebra also has stripes. A zebra looks like a horse. It lives in Africa. It is white with black stripes. Animals, like lions, hunt zebras. The stripes make the zebra hard to see. When a lion comes, all the zebras run away. The lion can't catch them. All the lion sees is lots of stripes.

Name ______________________ Date ____________

Comprehension Assessment

1. A tiger and a zebra are alike because they both

- ○ are brown
- ○ have stripes
- ○ like to hunt.

2. Where do tigers live?

- ○ in India
- ○ in Africa
- ○ in America

3. A tiger is

- ○ easy to see
- ○ very small
- ○ hard to see

4. Lions like to hunt

- ○ zebras
- ○ tigers
- ○ fish

5. This story is mostly about

- ○ hunting
- ○ Africa
- ○ animals

Name ______________________________ Date ____________

Vocabulary Assessment

Read the sentences. Fill in the space beside the word that fits best in the blank. Be sure to look at the words carefully and think about what they mean.

1. We will have a picnic at ____________ school.
   ○ our ○ are
2. Ellen will ____________ juice for us.
   ○ by ○ buy
3. We stopped playing because it was ____________.
   ○ darkest ○ darker ○ dark

Read the sentences. Fill in the space beside the word that fits best in the blank. Be sure to use the meaning of the sentence to choose your answer.

4. The water in the lake was ____________. Which word means the water was not warm?
   ○ cold ○ deep ○ clean
5. There were ____________ clouds in the sky. Which word means there were lots of clouds in the sky?
   ○ few ○ no ○ many

Read the question. Fill in the space beside the answer you think is best.

6. Fill in the space beside the word that has the prefix *un*.
   ○ under ○ untie ○ until
7. Fill in the space beside the word that has the prefix *re*.
   ○ reach ○ ready ○ refill
8. Fill in the space beside the word that has the prefix *dis*.
   ○ dislike ○ dishes ○ distant

Name ______________________________ Date ____________

Skills Assessment

Write the plural form of each word

1. mouse ____________ 3. penny ____________

2. house ____________ 4. beach ____________

Read the sentences. Draw a line under each adjective. Draw a circle around each adverb.

5. The black cat jumped quickly onto the bed. It walked carefully to the soft pillow. The cat curled up in a tiny ball and took a nap.

Read the sentences. Fill in the circle beside the word that tells what kind of sentence it is. Put the right punctuation mark at the end of each sentence.

6. Look out for that ice
   ○ statement ○ question ○ shows strong feeling

7. How long did the game last
   ○ statement ○ question ○ shows strong feeling

8. The coat you are wearing is pretty
   ○ statement ○ question ○ shows strong feeling

Read the sentences. Fill in the space beside the sentence that has correct punctuation.

9. ○ "What time is it?" asked Fred.

10. ○ Sue answered, It is about nine o'clock.

Read the sentences. Fill in the space beside the sentence in which the subject and verb are correct.

11. ○ Rabbits likes to eat carrots.

12. ○ My friends ride their bikes after school.

Oral Word Reading Assessment

1	bat	action	rain	first	hot
2	joyous	chase	trip	general	until
3	other	nurse	little	cow	weight
4	about	but	led	nature	say
5	tension	allowed	spoil	wrist	moon

Student Record: Oral Word Reading Assessment

Name ______________________________ Date ______________

1	bat	action	rain	first	hot
2	joyous	chase	trip	general	until
3	other	nurse	little	cow	weight
4	about	but	led	nature	say
5	tension	allowed	spoil	wrist	moon

Directions: Have the students read each word slowly. They should begin at the top-left and move from left to right, sweeping back to the beginning of the next row of words after finishing the last word in a row. You may stop the assessment if you sense that the student is becoming frustrated or if the student fails to read three consecutive words correctly.

Scoring: Draw a line through each word that the student reads incorrectly. If possible, circle or underline the letters that are the source of the error. It will be helpful to phonetically write the mispronunciation for any incorrect word. This information may be useful in identifying the areas in which a student needs additional instruction or practice. In the space below, write the number of words the student attempted and the number read correctly.

Words Attempted: ______ **Words Correct:** ______ **Percent Correct:** ______

Oral Fluency Assessment

After school, Marie went for a walk near her home. She found a funny looking rock. It had a shell in it. This surprised Marie. She lived very far from the ocean. Marie brought the stone home. Her mother said it was a fossil. She said that long ago, an ocean covered the place where they lived. When the animal in the shell died, the shell was covered with mud. The ocean dried up and the mud turned to stone. The shell Marie found was very, very old. She could not wait to go to school to tell her friends.

Student Record: Oral Fluency Assessment

Name ______________________________ Date ______________

After school, Marie went for a walk near her home. She found a funny looking rock. It had a shell in it. This surprised Marie. She lived very far from the ocean. Marie brought the stone home. Her mother said it was a fossil. She said that long ago, an ocean covered the place where they lived. When the animal in the shell died, the shell was covered with mud. The ocean dried up and the mud turned to stone. The shell Marie found was very, very old. She could not wait to go to school to tell her friends.

	Error Count	**Error Total**
Inserting an extra word	______________	(______)
Omitting a word	______________	(______)
Substituting words	______________	(______)
Refusing to attempt a word	______________	(______)
Mispronouncing a word	______________	(______)
Repeating a word	______________	(______)
Reversing words	______________	(______)
(0-3 errors=independent; 4-6 errors=instructional; 7+errors=frustration)	**Total:**	**(______)**

What is your estimation of this student's ability to read this text with fluency, accuracy, pacing, intonation, expression, and understanding? Circle the number that best reflects your estimation.

Below Average for this grade		Average for this grade		Above Average for this grade
1	2	3	4	5

Comprehension Assessment

The children went to the science museum. They saw a huge skeleton. It was from a dinosaur. It had lived a long time ago.

"That is a really big dinosaur," said Tomas.

"Yes," said Nick. "It's huge."

"I don't know," said Carol. "Is that the biggest dinosaur, Ms. Monroe?"

Ms. Monroe looked at the sign and said, "This dinosaur was pretty big. It was about 50 feet tall. It wasn't the biggest."

"Was this dinosaur mean? Did it eat other dinosaurs?" asked Wally. He was always asking questions.

"I think this dinosaur ate plants," said Ms. Monroe.

Then the children walked down the hall. They saw other bones. They also saw pictures of other dinosaurs. One had three horns. Another had a bill like a duck. They even saw dinosaur eggs.

Name ________________________ Date ______________

Comprehension Assessment

1. What kind of museum was it?

- ○ art
- ○ science
- ○ music

2. The skeleton was a

- ○ dinosaur
- ○ elephant
- ○ whale

3. The last things the children saw were

- ○ plants
- ○ bones
- ○ eggs

4. Who was always asking questions?

- ○ Wally
- ○ Nick
- ○ Carol

5. Another word for really big is

- ○ pretty
- ○ huge
- ○ about

Name ______________________________ Date ______________

Vocabulary Assessment

Read the sentences. Draw a circle around the compound word in each sentence. A compound word is made up of two smaller words.

1. The family took a vacation on a houseboat.

2. Bev's father went to sleep in the armchair.

3. At the end of the trail was a beautiful waterfall.

Read the sentences. In the blank, write the correct form of the adjective in parentheses.

4. The kitchen is the (warm) ______________ spot in our house.

5. The lawn is (green) ______________ this year than last year.

6. The lion in the zoo was (loud) ______________ than the tiger.

7. The third problem was the (easy) ______________ on the test.

Read the words. Draw a circle around the word in which only the root word is underlined.

8. replay replay replay

9. deepest deepest deepest

10. reading reading reading

Name ________________________________ Date ______________

Skills Assessment

Read the sentences. Fill in the space beside the sentence that has correct punctuation.

1. ○ Prizes will be given for first, second and, third place.
2. ○ The new store sells bikes skis and snowboards.
3. ○ Our library has books, magazines, and newspapers.

Read the sentences. Fill in the space beside the answer that tells if it has a compound subject or compound predicate.

4. Mary and Cathy joined the swimming team.

   ○ compound subject ○ compound predicate

5. Gina rose and walked to the front of the room.

   ○ compound subject ○ compound predicate

6. The bus turned the corner and stopped near the school.

   ○ compound subject ○ compound predicate

7. Ice and snow fell from the roof onto the sidewalk.

   ○ compound subject ○ compound predicate

Read the sentences. In the blank, write the correct abbreviation for the word in parentheses.

8. My aunt lives on Market (street) ______________.
9. The children visited (mister) ____________ Stanley.
10. (Doctor) ______________ Smith lives here.
11. Kendra walked down Fifth (Avenue) ____________.
12. Our school is on Willow (Road) ______________.

Oral Word Reading Assessment

1	she	after	sky	magic	so
2	three	pie	home	now	boy
3	belief	girl	decide	right	nice
4	these	hurry	chew	goes	using
5	team	like	slow	going	huge
6	movie	jet	house	coat	cycle

Student Record: Oral Word Reading Assessment

Name ______________________________ **Date** ______________

1	she	after	sky	magic	so
2	three	pie	home	now	boy
3	belief	girl	decide	right	nice
4	these	hurry	chew	goes	using
5	team	like	slow	going	huge
6	movie	jet	house	coat	cycle

Directions: Have the students read each word slowly. They should begin at the top-left and move from left to right, sweeping back to the beginning of the next row of words after finishing the last word in a row. You may stop the assessment if you sense that the student is becoming frustrated or if the student fails to read three consecutive words correctly.

Scoring: Draw a line through each word that the student reads incorrectly. If possible, circle or underline the letters that are the source of the error. It will be helpful to phonetically write the mispronunciation for any incorrect word. This information may be useful in identifying the areas in which a student needs additional instruction or practice. In the space below, write the number of words the student attempted and the number read correctly.

Words Attempted: ______ **Words Correct:** ______ **Percent Correct:** ______

Oral Fluency Assessment

Sally and Jack saw the little kitten in the tree. They went into the house and told their mother. The three of them went to the basement. They got a long ladder. They took the ladder to the yard and put it on a branch of the tree. Jack and Sally held the ladder. Mother went up and got the kitten. She was very careful so she did not get hurt. Mother came down with the kitten. It was very happy to be on the ground again. The kitten purred and purred. Mother said Sally and Jack had been brave.

Student Record: Oral Fluency Assessment

Name ______________________________ Date ______________

Sally and Jack saw the little kitten in the tree. They went into the house and told their mother. The three of them went to the basement. They got a long ladder. They took the ladder to the yard and put it on a branch of the tree. Jack and Sally held the ladder. Mother went up and got the kitten. She was very careful so she did not get hurt. Mother came down with the kitten. It was very happy to be on the ground again. The kitten purred and purred. Mother said Sally and Jack had been brave.

	Error Count	Error Total
Inserting an extra word	______________	(_____)
Omitting a word	______________	(_____)
Substituting words	______________	(_____)
Refusing to attempt a word	______________	(_____)
Mispronouncing a word	______________	(_____)
Repeating a word	______________	(_____)
Reversing words	______________	(_____)
(0-3 errors=independent; 4-6 errors=instructional; 7+errors=frustration)	**Total:**	**(_____)**

What is your estimation of this student's ability to read this text with fluency, accuracy, pacing, intonation, expression, and understanding? Circle the number that best reflects your estimation.

Below Average for this grade		Average for this grade		Above Average for this grade
1	2	3	4	5

Comprehension Assessment

"What's wrong, Ollie?" Mr. Miller spoke softly to his son.

"I think I made a big mistake, Dad." Ollie looked down as he spoke. He had a funny feeling in his tummy.

Mrs. Miller walked into the room. She heard what Ollie said.

"It can be that bad, can it?" she asked.

"Well," answered Ollie, "I picked some flowers from Mr. Lake's garden. I gave them to my teacher. She liked them a lot. I feel bad because I didn't ask Mr. Lake. I just took them."

"I see," said Mr. Miller. "That is a pretty big mistake. What do you think we should do?"

Ollie looked at his parents. "I think I should go to see Mr. Lake. I should tell him what happened."

"That's a good idea," said Mrs. Miller. "Do you want us to go with you?"

"No," said Ollie. "I did it myself. I should go myself and say I'm sorry."

Ollie left the house and ran next door to talk to Mr. Lake. His mom and dad watched through the window. Mr. Lake shook Ollie's hand, then Ollie came back home.

"Mom! Dad! Mr. Lake wasn't mad. He said I had courage to tell him. He said I could make it up by helping in the garden." Ollie was out of breath, but he was happy. He could tell from the way that his parents looked that they were proud of him.

Name ______________________ Date ____________

Comprehension Assessment

1. This story is most like
- ○ a real story
- ○ a fairy tale
- ○ a poem

2. Why does Ollie's tummy feel funny?
- ○ He ran home from school too fast.
- ○ He ate too much.
- ○ He knows he did something wrong.

3. The mistake Ollie made was
- ○ giving flowers to his teacher
- ○ not asking Mr. Lake
- ○ leaving school early

4. Ollie's parents are proud because he
- ○ always does his homework
- ○ knows that people like flowers
- ○ told Mr. Lake he was sorry

5. If someone has courage, they are
- ○ foolish
- ○ brave
- ○ careful

Name ____________________ Date ____________

Vocabulary Assessment

Read the sentences. Fill in the space beside the word that means the same as the underlined word.

1. The boat sailed across the lake.
   ○ box ○ raft ○ ship
2. Jeff carried a sack of groceries.
   ○ box ○ bag ○ basket
3. The tiger dashed into the jungle.
   ○ ran ○ jumped ○ crawled

Read the sentences. Fill in the space beside the word that fits best in both sentences.

4. The plane will ____________ soon.
   The farmer grew corn on her ____________.
   ○ arrive ○ land ○ farm
5. Did you put your money in the ____________?
   Trees grew on the ____________ of the stream.
   ○ bank ○ wallet ○ side

Read the question. Fill in the space beside the answer that means the opposite of the underlined word.

6. George filled the bottle with water.
   ○ emptied ○ poured ○ washed
7. A tiny bird sat on the branch.
   ○ pretty ○ rare ○ huge
8. The bed was too soft for me.
   ○ few ○ hard ○ high

Name ________________________________ Date ______________

Skills Assessment

Read the sentences. Draw a line under each position word.

1. Brian swam under the boat. Sue looked over the side to see where he was. He surprised her by coming up quickly.

Read the sentences. Put commas in the right place in each sentence.

2. The park had many trees shrubs and bushes.
3. We will have a test in spelling math and science.
4. Leaves sticks and branches were all over after the storm.

Read the sentences. Draw a line under each common noun. Draw a circle around each proper noun.

5. On Saturday, we will have a party. It is his birthday. We want to surprise him. His parents are giving him skis. They will go skiing in December.

Read the sentences. Draw a line under each adjective. Draw a circle around each adverb.

6. A long pile of rocks went into the water. The waves crashed loudly against it. We walked carefully on the slippery stones.

Read the sentences. In the blank, write the possessive form of the word in parentheses.

7. A (bear) ________________ claws can be three inches long.
8. A stone cracked our (car) ______________ windshield.

Read the letter. In the blank, write the correct form of the words in parentheses. Don't forget the punctuation marks.

9. (dear sammy) ________________

I can't wait until we visit next week. Going fishing is one of the first things I want to do. I hope the weather is good.

10. (your cousin) ________________

Roberto

Oral Word Reading Assessment

1	mat	block	clam	shirt	taught
2	bring	during	huge	train	desk
3	might	fall	flew	thought	find
4	cut	true	bike	scratch	wrong
5	while	fault	zoo	sock	from
6	fur	luck	grade	these	lie
7	walk	far	net	always	never

Student Record: Oral Word Reading Assessment

Name ______________________________ **Date** ____________

1	mat	block	clam	shirt	taught
2	bring	during	huge	train	desk
3	might	fall	flew	thought	find
4	cut	true	bike	scratch	wrong
5	while	fault	zoo	sock	from
6	fur	luck	grade	these	lie
7	walk	far	net	always	never

Directions: Have the students read each word slowly. They should begin at the top-left and move from left to right, sweeping back to the beginning of the next row of words after finishing the last word in a row. You may stop the assessment if you sense that the student is becoming frustrated or if the student fails to read three consecutive words correctly.

Scoring: Draw a line through each word that the student reads incorrectly. If possible, circle or underline the letters that are the source of the error. It will be helpful to phonetically write the mispronunciation for any incorrect word. This information may be useful in identifying the areas in which a student needs additional instruction or practice. In the space below, write the number of words the student attempted and the number read correctly.

Words Attempted: ______ **Words Correct:** ______ **Percent Correct:** ______

Oral Fluency Assessment

Frank liked his grandmother's stories. He could listen to them all day. She talked about things that happened long ago. Grandmother could remember everything. She often showed the children pictures in a scrapbook when she told stories. She told Frank and the other children stories about their family. The children liked the stories about their parents the best. Grandmother told the children about the games their parents played. She told them about the clothes they used to wear. She said things were very different long ago. The children said she was right. They were happy with the way things are today.

Student Record: Oral Fluency Assessment

Name ______________________ **Date** ____________

Frank liked his grandmother's stories. He could listen to them all day. She talked about things that happened long ago. Grandmother could remember everything. She often showed the children pictures in a scrapbook when she told stories. She told Frank and the other children stories about their family. The children liked the stories about their parents the best. Grandmother told the children about the games their parents played. She told them about the clothes they used to wear. She said things were very different long ago. The children said she was right. They were happy with the way things are today.

	Error Count	Error Total
Inserting an extra word	______	(____)
Omitting a word	______	(____)
Substituting words	______	(____)
Refusing to attempt a word	______	(____)
Mispronouncing a word	______	(____)
Repeating a word	______	(____)
Reversing words	______	(____)
(0-3 errors=independent; 4-6 errors=instructional; 7+errors=frustration)	**Total:**	**(____)**

What is your estimation of this student's ability to read this text with fluency, accuracy, pacing, intonation, expression, and understanding? Circle the number that best reflects your estimation.

Below Average for this grade		Average for this grade		Above Average for this grade
1	2	3	4	5

Comprehension Assessment

Nat loved to write. He always had a paper and pencil with him. Now he had something fun to write about. His family was moving. They were traveling west on the Oregon Trail.

The Oregon Trail was used by many people long ago. It was 2,000 miles long. The trail went across the mountains to the ocean. Nat's parents bought a covered wagon for the trip. The wagon was called a prairie schooner. Nathaniel asked his father about the name. His father told him the wagon was named after a boat. The white cover of the wagon looked like the sails of a boat. A schooner is a kind of boat. The land on which they traveled was a prairie.

The family was part of a wagon train. Many wagons moved together. Traveling together gave them protection. It was a good idea to travel together. The people could help one another.

On the trip, Nat helped his parents in many ways. He would cut wood and carry water. One day, they had to cross a river. Nathaniel had to get into the water to move the wagon across.

When they reached Oregon, Nat was happy. He never forgot his trip. When he grew up, he would often look at his journal.

Name ______________________ Date ____________

Comprehension Assessment

1. What did Nat probably do every day?
   - ○ go to school
   - ○ write in his journal
   - ○ play sports with friends

2. From the story, you know that a schooner is a kind of
   - ○ boat
   - ○ chair
   - ○ horse

3. When they reached Oregon, Nathaniel was
   - ○ upset
   - ○ happy
   - ○ hungry

4. Which of these is true about the Oregon Trail?
   - ○ It was for boats.
   - ○ No one could find it.
   - ○ Many people traveled on it.

5. People traveled in wagon trains mostly for
   - ○ protection
   - ○ fun
   - ○ speed

Name ______________________________ Date ______________

Vocabulary Assessment

Read each sentence. Fill in the blank with the correct word from the homophones in parentheses.

1. A ranger (lead/led) __________ the children through the park.

2. This metal is so heavy it must be (lead/led) __________ .

3. Last week, (our/hour) __________ dog had puppies.

4. The movie will begin in one (our/hour) __________.

5. The answer to the problem is (ate/eight) __________ .

6. We (ate/eight) __________ pizza for dinner.

Read the sentences. Fill in the space beside the word that has the same root word as the underlined word in the sentence.

7. The Miller family has <u>lived</u> in our town more than 100 years.

○ glove ○ shovel ○ alive

8. The <u>handle</u> of the cup is broken.

○ handful ○ sandy ○ honest

9. The workers <u>replaced</u> the broken motor.

○ package ○ placing ○ playful

Read the words. Fill in the space beside the compound word in each group.

10. ○ peaceful ○ vegetable ○ morning ○ houseboat

11. ○ window ○ television ○ daylight ○ elephant

12. ○ carried ○ snowflake ○ dinner ○ package

Name ______________________________ Date ______________

Skills Assessment

Read the sentences. Fill in the space beside each answer that is a compound sentence.

1. ○ The doorbell rang, and the dogs started barking.
2. ○ Movie stars and athletes are usually famous.
3. ○ The pool is open, but it is too cold to swim.

Read the sentences. Fill in the space beside the sentence in which the subject and verb agree.

4. ○ A new store are coming to our town.
   ○ The children meets their parents at the bus stop.
   ○ Hikers often climb the hill near our school.
5. ○ Trains leave the station every hour.
   ○ A lion sleep after it eats.
   ○ A computer cost less than before.

Read the sentences. In the blank, write the correct past-tense form of the verb in parentheses.

6. My sister (catch) ____________ a cold last week.
7. The worker (paint) ____________ the house yesterday.
8. Some ducks (fly) ____________ over the house earlier.

Read the sentences. Draw a line under each <u>possessive noun</u> that should have an apostrophe.

9. This books author is from our town.
10. Our class met our teachers father.

Teacher's Annotated Blackline Masters and Assessment

Name ____________ Date ________

BLM 2 Grammar (Common and Proper Nouns)

Read the story and circle the nouns that should begin with a capital letter. Write the noun correctly above each circle. Then write the story correctly on the lines below.

Ellen

ellen is going to the beach. She is going to see

Pacific Ocean

the pacific ocean for the first time. Ellen's friend

Marie Fluffy

marie is going with her. Ellen's dog fluffy has to stay home. Grandma made lunch for the trip. The girls will share their stories when they get

Sunday May

home on sunday, may 20.

Ellen is going to the beach.

She is going to see the Pacific Ocean for the first time.

Ellen's friend Marie is going with her.

Ellen's dog Fluffy has to stay home.

Grandma made lunch for the trip.

The girls will share their stories when they get home on Sunday, May 20.

Name ____________ Date ________

BLM 2 Grammar (Subject-Verb Agreement)

Read the story and circle the correct verb for each sentence. Then write each sentence correctly on the lines below.

Kit (get, gets) up in class to tell her story. All the children (sit, sits) around the room. Kit (open, opens) her mouth. They (hear, hears) no sound. Kit's face (turn, turns) red. She (start, starts) to laugh. Then Kit (sit, sits) down.

1. Kit gets up in class to tell her story.
2. All the children sit around the room.
3. Kit opens her mouth.
4. They hear no sound.
5. Kit's face turns red.
6. She starts to laugh.
7. Then Kit sits down.

Name ____________ Date ________

BLM 2 Grammar (Pronouns and Antecedents)

Read the story and circle the incorrect pronouns. Write the correct pronoun above each circle. Then write the story correctly on the lines below.

Karen's mom likes to read to Karen at

She

bedtime. He curls up on the bed with Karen and

She

Karen's cat, Pete. He reads even if Karen falls

her

asleep. Sometimes our cat is the only one

him

awake. Karen's mom just keeps reading to her.

he

Pete knows a good story when she hears one.

Karen's mom likes to read to Karen at bedtime.

She curls up on the bed with Karen and Karen's cat, Pete.

She reads even if Karen falls asleep.

Sometimes her cat is the only one awake.

Karen's mom just keeps reading to him.

Pete knows a good story when he hears one.

Name ____________ Date ________

BLM 2 Grammar (Adjectives)

Read the story and choose an adjective from the following list to complete each sentence. Write the word on the line. Then write the story on the lines below.

tasty	big	new	steep
rusty	broken	three	green

Answers may vary.

I rode my bike to the children's library. I parked it in the __rusty__ rack and walked up the __steep__ steps. Then I opened the __big__ door and met the __new__ librarian. I picked out __three__ books. It was a hard choice. I put the books in my __green__ pack with a __broken__ zipper. Then I rode home, ate a __tasty__ sandwich, and started reading.

I rode my bike to the children's library. I parked it in the rusty rack and walked up the steep steps. Then I opened the big door and met the new librarian. I picked out three books. It was a hard choice. I put the books in my green pack with a broken zipper. Then I rode home, ate a tasty sandwich, and started reading.

Name ______________________ Date __________

BLM 2 Grammar (Proper Nouns)

Read the story and circle the proper nouns that should start with a capital letter. Write the noun correctly above each circle. Then write the story correctly on the lines below.

Mark Twain was a writer. He was one of America's america's best storytellers. His real name was Samuel Clemens clemens. When he was a child, he lived in Hannibal, Missouri missouri. He wrote about life on the Mississippi mississippi River. One of his most famous books is called Tom *tom Sawyer*.

Mark Twain was a writer. He was one of America's best storytellers. His real name was Samuel Clemens. When he was a child, he lived in Hannibal, Missouri. He wrote about life on the Mississippi River. One of his most famous books is called *Tom Sawyer*.

Name ______________________ Date __________

BLM 2 Grammar (End Punctuation)

Read the story and circle the incorrect end marks. Write the correct end mark above each circle. Then write the story correctly on the lines below.

Jeff's dad is a writer. He has written about a hundred books. Have you ever read any of them? I have read some of his adventure stories. Jeff's dad travels to interesting places to get ideas. Writing takes a lot of time, but it seems like a great job.

Jeff's dad is a writer.

He has written about a hundred books. (or !)

Have you ever read any of them?

I have read some of his adventure stories.

Jeff's dad travels to interesting places to get ideas.

Writing takes a lot of time, but it seems like a great job.

Name ______________________ Date __________

BLM 2 Grammar (Pronouns and Antecedents)

Read the story and circle the incorrect pronouns. Write the correct pronoun above each circle. Then write the story correctly on the lines below.

Pete's dog, Maggie, brings him them all kinds of things. She has brought him it five bones, three balls, and six shoes. Pete never knows what she they will bring home next. But he doesn't really care. He She just wants Maggie to be happy. And she is! Maggie knows that Pete will love her him no matter what she he brings home.

Pete's dog, Maggie, brings him all kinds of things.

She has brought him five bones, three balls, and six shoes.

Pete never knows what she will bring home next.

But he doesn't really care.

He just wants Maggie to be happy.

And she is!

Maggie knows that Pete will love her no matter what she brings home.

Name ______________________ Date __________

BLM 2 Grammar (Types of Sentences: Capitalization and End Punctuation)

Read the story and circle the incorrect end marks. Also circle words that should begin with a capital letter. Write the correct end mark or capital letter above each circle. Then write each sentence correctly on the lines below.

M mrs. Reed met a rabbit in her garden and told it to scat. But do you know what the rabbit did? T the rabbit showed her a pile of weeds.

"For three carrots I will weed your garden," he said.

"W what a deal!" Mrs. Reed thought. N now Mrs. Reed's garden is weed free.

1. Mrs. Reed met a rabbit in her garden and told it to scat.
2. But do you know what the rabbit did?
3. The rabbit showed her a pile of weeds.
4. "For three carrots I will weed your garden," he said.
5. "What a deal!" Mrs. Reed thought.
6. Now Mrs. Reed's garden is weed free.

Name ______________________ Date __________

BLM 2 Grammar (Verbs: Irregular)

Read the story and circle the incorrect verbs. Write the correct verb above each circle. Then write the story correctly on the lines below.

Last week, I have [had] to clean out my garage. I get [got] a family of squirrels to help me. They swept and mopped every inch. They throw [threw] away a stack of junk. They do [did] a lot of work, so I gave them some lemonade and cookies. We make [made] a great team!

Last week, I had to clean out my garage.

I got a family of squirrels to help me.

They swept and mopped every inch.

They threw away a stack of junk.

They did a lot of work, so I gave them some lemonade and cookies.

We made a great team!

Name ______________________ Date __________

BLM 2 Grammar (Punctuating Sentences)

Read the story and circle the incorrect end marks. Write the correct end mark above each circle. Then write the story correctly on the lines below.

My friend told me to go see the unicorn at the zoo. He said that the zookeeper found it and put it in a safe place! [.]

"No way!" I said. But I had to go see for myself. I went to the zoo and couldn't believe my eyes? [!] Did you know that unicorns have purple eyes. [?] Well neither did I? [!]

My friend told me to go see the unicorn at the zoo.

He said that the zookeeper found it and put it in a safe place.

"No way!" I said.

But I had to go see for myself.

I went to the zoo and couldn't believe my eyes! (or .)

Did you know that unicorns have purple eyes?

Well neither did I. (or !)

Name ______________________ Date __________

BLM 2 Grammar (Pronouns and Antecedents)

Read the story and circle the incorrect pronouns. Write the correct pronoun above each circle. Then write the story correctly on the lines below.

Matt was taking a walk on the beach when she [he] heard something strange. It sounded to them [him] like a crying baby. Then he looked all around and spotted an otter. It had gotten his [its] flipper stuck under a log. Matt couldn't move the log alone, so they [he] got some friends to help him. She [They] rolled the log away and set the otter free.

Matt was taking a walk on the beach when he heard something strange.

It sounded to him like a crying baby.

Then he looked all around and spotted an otter.

It had gotten its flipper stuck under a log.

Matt couldn't move the log alone, so he got some friends to help him.

They rolled the log away and set the otter free.

Name ______________________ Date __________

BLM 2 Grammar (Possessive Nouns)

Read the story and circle the words that need an apostrophe. Write the correct word above each circle. Then write the story correctly on the lines below.

Jays [Jay's] summer job is walking dogs. He picks them up at his neighbors [neighbors'] houses every day. Then he heads for the park. Jay knows all of the dogs [dogs'] likes and dislikes. Mrs. Changs [Chang's] dog does not like to get his feet wet. Mr. Gordons [Gordon's] dog likes to ride in Jays [Jay's] backpack. Lucky likes to chew on Boomers [Boomer's] collar when they all stop to rest.

Jay's summer job is walking dogs. He picks them up at his neighbors' houses every day. Then he heads for the park. Jay knows all of the dogs' likes and dislikes. Mrs. Chang's dog does not like to get his feet wet. Mr. Gordon's dog likes to ride in Jay's backpack. Lucky likes to chew on Boomer's collar when they all stop to rest.

Name ____________ Date ________

BLM 2 Grammar (Types of Sentences: End Punctuation)

Read the story and circle the incorrect end marks. Write the correct end mark above each circle. Then write the story correctly on the lines below.

Once upon a time, there was a king(!) He was very unhappy because he could not leave his castle(?) One day, a bright red bird flew in the king's window and sang a song(?)

The king smiled and said, "I wish I felt as happy and free as you do."

And do you know what happened(.) Poof(.) The king and the bird flew away together(?)

Once upon a time, there was a king. He was very unhappy because he could not leave his castle. One day, a bright red bird flew in the king's window and sang a song.

The king smiled and said, "I wish I felt as happy and free as you do."

And do you know what happened? Poof! The king and the bird flew away together. (or !)

Name ____________ Date ________

BLM 2 Grammar (Subject-Verb Agreement in Simple Sentences)

Read the story and circle the incorrect verbs. Write the correct verb above each circle. Then write the story correctly on the lines below.

Ned races over to Dan's house whenever it snows. Dan (have) [has] a big hill next to his house. It (are) [is] the best sledding hill around. Children (comes) [come] from miles away to sled down Dan's hill. Mothers and fathers (watches) [watch] and take pictures. Everyone (have) [has] a great time!

Ned races over to Dan's house whenever it snows. Dan has a big hill next to his house. It is the best sledding hill around. Children come from miles away to sled down Dan's hill. Mothers and fathers watch and take pictures. Everyone has a great time!

Name ____________ Date ________

BLM 2 Grammar (Types of Sentences)

Read the story and circle incorrect end marks or add missing end marks. Write the correct end mark above each circle. Then write the story correctly on the lines below.

Some animals have special coloring in the winter. They turn white. They blend in with the snow and ice( ) You can't even see them! Some wolves and rabbits change from tan or gray to white(?) A red fox in winter looks as white as this paper(?) Polar bears stay white all the time( ) After all, they live in snow all year round!

Some animals have special coloring in the winter. They turn white. They blend in with the snow and ice. You can't even see them! (or.) Some wolves and rabbits change from tan or gray to white. A red fox in winter looks as white as this paper. Polar bears stay white all the time. After all, they live in snow all year round! (or .)

Name ____________ Date ________

BLM 2 Grammar (Adverbs)

Read the story and choose an adverb from the following list to complete each sentence. Write the word on the line. Then write the story on the lines below.

sharply	deeply	softly
quietly	closely	quickly

Answers may vary.

The wolf is an interesting animal. The colors of a wolf's fur __softly__ blend from head to toe. Look __closely__ to see tan fur turn to brown. Gray fur __quickly__ changes from silver to blue. A wolf looks __sharply__ with eyes that glow like gold. It sniffs __deeply__ with its black nose. Look! There's a wolf watching __quietly__ from behind a tree.

The wolf is an interesting animal. The colors of a wolf's fur softly blend from head to toe. Look closely to see tan fur turn to brown. Gray fur quickly changes from silver to blue. A wolf looks sharply with eyes that glow like gold. It sniffs deeply with its black nose. Look! There's a wolf watching quietly from behind a tree.

Name ______________________ Date ____________

BLM 2 Grammar (Adverbs and Adjectives)

Read the story. Then circle the adjectives and underline the adverbs. Write each adjective and adverb under the correct head below.

A small, green worm was crawling slowly along a leaf. A big hawk flapped its wings wildly. It landed on a brown log near the leaf. The hawk stared at the leaf with glassy eyes. The tiny worm suddenly stopped and waited. The hawk looked closely. But it did not see the little worm. What luck! The hawk left.

Adjectives	Adverbs
small	slowly
green	wildly
big	suddenly
brown	closely
glassy	
tiny	
little	

Name ______________________ Date ____________

BLM 2 Grammar (Punctuating Dialogue)

Read the story and put an arrow where quotation marks should be. Write quotation marks above each arrow. Then write the story correctly on the lines below.

A bobcat chased a rabbit. The rabbit dove into a pond.

"A little water won't stop me," said the bobcat.

"Look out for your spots!" yelled the rabbit.

The bobcat stopped. He looked surprised.

"What do you mean?" asked the bobcat.

"You don't want to wash off your spots," said the rabbit. "That's why cats don't like water!"

A bobcat chased a rabbit. The rabbit dove into a pond.

"A little water won't stop me," said the bobcat.

"Look out for your spots!" yelled the rabbit.

The bobcat stopped. He looked surprised.

"What do you mean?" asked the bobcat.

"You don't want to wash off your spots," said the rabbit.

"That's why cats don't like water!"

Name ______________________ Date ____________

BLM 2 Grammar (Nouns)

Read the story and choose a noun from the following list to complete each sentence. Write the noun on the line. Then write each sentence correctly on the lines below.

nest	yard	pond	lawn
deck	goose	Mrs. Chan	crows

Answers may vary.

Mr. Chan has a pond in his yard. A goose from Canada swims there. A flock of crows hops on the lawn. A robin is building a nest in a hollow tree. Mrs. Chan put a feeder out on the deck. The Chans have a busy, noisy yard.

1. Mr. Chan has a pond in his yard.
2. A goose from Canada swims there.
3. A flock of crows hops on the lawn.
4. A robin is building a nest in a hollow tree.
5. Mrs. Chan put a feeder out on the deck.
6. The Chans have a busy, noisy yard.

Name ______________________ Date ____________

BLM 2 Grammar (Commas in a Series)

Read the story and insert an arrow wherever a comma is needed. Place a comma above each arrow. Then write the story correctly on the lines below.

It is fun to hunt for fossils. They can be found in frozen soil, old creek beds, and lakes. You might find a fossil of a footprint, a fern, or a bone. An animal's organs, hair, and skin disappear quickly. They are not saved over time.

It is fun to hunt for fossils. They can be found in frozen soil, old creek beds, and lakes. You might find a fossil of a footprint, a fern, or a bone. An animal's organs, hair, and skin disappear quickly. They are not saved over time.

Name ______________________ Date __________

BLM 2 Grammar (Abbreviations)

Read the story and circle the incorrect abbreviations. Write the correct abbreviation above each circle. Then write the story correctly on the lines below.

Once a year Mtr. (Mr.) Gonzalez goes to the doctor for a checkup. Dtr. (Dr.) Mason has an office downtown on Elm Str. (St.) Afterwards, Mr. Gonzalez likes to stop for a snack. He goes to a place called the Snack Shack on Second Av. (Ave.) Then he heads for home on a bus that leaves every Mond. (Mon.) at five.

Once a year Mr. Gonzalez goes to the doctor for a checkup. Dr. Mason has an office downtown on Elm St. Afterwards, Mr. Gonzalez likes to stop for a snack. He goes to a place called the Snack Shack on Second Ave. Then he heads for home on a bus that leaves every Mon. at five.

Name ______________________ Date __________

BLM 2 Grammar (Compound Subjects and Predicates)

Read the story and underline the compound subjects. Circle the compound predicates. Then write each compound subject and compound predicate under the correct head.

Heavy rain and snowfall can cause flooding. Lakes and rivers fill up and spill over. The water floods farmland and destroys crops. Sometimes roads and bridges must be closed. Too much water can cause damage and make some places unsafe.

Compound Subjects

Heavy rain and snowfall

Lakes and rivers

roads and bridges

Compound Predicates

fill up and spill over

floods farmland and destroys crops

can cause damage and make some places unsafe

Name ______________________ Date __________

BLM 2 Grammar (Subject-Verb Agreement)

Read the story and circle the incorrect verbs. Write the correct verb above each circle. Then write the story correctly on the lines below.

Rabbit tracks is (are) easy to spot in the snow. They are so different from other animal tracks. A rabbit land (lands) flat on its back feet. Those tracks is (are) long. A rabbit barely touch (touches) its front feet to the ground. The front feet makes (make) small prints. These different prints tells (tell) us the rabbit's direction.

Rabbit tracks are easy to spot in the snow. They are so different from other animal tracks. A rabbit lands flat on its back feet. Those tracks are long. A rabbit barely touches its front feet to the ground. The front feet make small prints. These different prints tell us the rabbit's direction.

Name ______________________ Date __________

BLM 2 Grammar (Letters: Form and Punctuation)

Read the letter and circle the capital letters and punctuation that are missing or incorrect. Write the correct letters or punctuation above each circle. Then write the letter correctly on the lines below.

january (D) 26 2001

dear (D) granny (G)

we're (W) having a great time at the beach? (.) what (W) shells we've collected (!) They come in so many different shapes and sizes (.) would (W) you like to help us sometime (?) we (W) would love to have you.

yours (Y) truly (,)

Jenny

January 26, 2001

Dear Granny,

We're having a great time at the beach. What shells we've collected! They come in so many different shapes and sizes. Would you like to help us sometime? We would love to have you.

Yours truly,

Jenny

Name ______________________ Date __________

BLM 2 Grammar (Verbs: Regular and Irregular)

Read the story and circle verbs that are not in the past tense. Write a past tense verb above each circle. Then write the story correctly on the lines below.

A dragon waded into the lake. The water feels (felt) so good. But the dragon become (became) stuck in the mud. Soon a knight walks (walked) by. The dragon waves (waved) for help. Then the knight helps the dragon.

A dragon waded into the lake.
The water felt so good.
But the dragon became stuck in the mud.
Soon a knight walked by.
The dragon waved for help.
Then the knight gave the dragon a hand.

Name ______________________ Date __________

BLM 2 Grammar (Possessive Nouns)

Read the story and circle the possessive nouns are not correct. Write the word correctly above each circle. Then write the story correctly on the lines below.

Kens' (Ken's) career began in Jan's workshop. Jan ran her dads' (dad's) wood shop with three carpenters. The carpenter's (carpenters') job was to build boats. Many other worker's (workers') skills were needed to make fine sailboats. Ken soon became Jans' best carpenter.

Ken's career began in Jan's workshop. Jan ran her dad's wood shop with three carpenters. The carpenters' job was to build boats. Many other workers' skills were needed to make fine sailboats. Ken soon became Jan's best carpenter.

Name ______________________ Date __________

BLM 2 Grammar (Letters: Form and Punctuation)

Read the letter and circle the capital letters and punctuation that are missing or incorrect. Write the correct letters or punctuation above each circle. Then write the letter correctly on the lines below.

june (J) 12 (,) 2001

Dear Mark,

we (W) are in Washington, D.C. visiting the Capital Building. Today, I met the senator from my state? (.) He used to work with my dad (.) what (W) a nice man he is (!)

I can't wait to tell you all about our trip! (.)

your (Y) friend (,)

Carly

June 12, 2001

Dear Mark,

We are on a tour of Washington, D.C. Today, I met the senator from my state. He used to work with my dad. What a nice man he is! I can't wait to tell you all about our trip.

Your friend,

Carly

Name ______________________ Date __________

BLM 2 Grammar (Commas in a Series)

Read the story and insert an arrow wherever a comma is needed. Place a comma above each arrow. Then write the story correctly on the lines below.

One day a little girl showed her mother a penny,^ a nickel,^ and a quarter.

"I was with Grandpa," said the little girl. "He gave me a penny for my thoughts. But I told him that they were worth more than a penny. So he smiled,^ laughed,^ and gave me a nickel. Then I told him that I was thinking,^ wishing,^ and hoping for a shiny quarter."

One day a little girl showed her mother a penny, a nickel, and a quarter.

"I was with Grandpa," said the little girl. "He gave me a penny for my thoughts. But I told him that they were worth more than a penny. So he smiled, laughed, and gave me a nickel. Then I told him that I was thinking, wishing, and hoping for a shiny quarter."

Name ______________________ Date __________

BLM 2 Grammar (Review Parts of Speech: Nouns, Adjectives, and Adverbs)

Read the story and underline the nouns, circle the adjectives, and draw a box around the adverbs. Then write each noun, adjective, and adverb under the correct head.

A young mother closely watched her playful child. The curious child crept slowly toward a tall bookcase. He gently touched a large book. The happy child sat quietly and turned the colorful pages.

Noun	Adjective	Adverb
mother	young	closely
child	playful	slowly
child	curious	gently
bookcase	tall	quietly
book	large	
child	happpy	
pages	colorful	

Name ______________________ Date __________

BLM 2 Grammar (Abbreviations)

Read the story and circle the incorrect abbreviations. Write the correct abbreviation above each circle. Then write the story on the lines below.

Michael delivers newspapers to people in his neighborhood. Every Sund. (Sun.) he takes a paper to Dtr. (Dr.) Sharma and Msr. (Mrs.) Boyle on Oak Str. (St.) Every Fry. (Fri.) he takes a paper to Mtr. (Mr.) Graham on Beech Av. (Ave.) In Sept., Michael will have delivered papers for three years.

Michael delivers newspapers to people in his neighborhood. Every Sun. he takes a paper to Dr. Sharma and Mrs. Boyle on Oak St. Every Fri. he takes a paper to Mr. Graham on Beech Ave. In Sept., Michael will have delivered papers for three years.

Name ______________________ Date __________

BLM 2 Grammar (Verbs: Regular and Irregular)

Read the story and circle the incorrect verbs. Write the correct past-tense verb above each circle. Then write the story correctly on the lines below.

Every day after school, Jack walkt (walked) his dog, Nikki. It was a chore. Nikki taked (took) her time and smelled everything along the way.

Then one day Jack thinked (thought) of a plan. He decide (decided) to take along another dog to make the walks more fun. The idea workt (worked) well. Nikki gotten (got) more exercise. They all have (had) more fun.

Every day after school, Zach walked his dog, Nikki. It was a chore. Nikki took her time and smelled everything along the way.

Then one day Zach thought of a plan. He decided to take along another dog to make the walks more fun. The idea worked well. Nikki got more exercise. They all had more fun.

Name ______________________ Date __________

BLM 2 Grammar (Commas in a Series)

Read the story and insert an arrow wherever a comma is needed. Place a comma above each arrow. Then write the sentences on the lines below.

Once a month, Moira goes into the city with her grandmother. She loves seeing all the traffic, the people, and the tall buildings. They ride a taxi past Third, Fourth, and Fifth Avenues. Then they stop at a large department store. Moira's grandmother wants to buy a dress, a pair of shoes, and a purse. Moira soon gets tired. She can't wait to get back in the car, drive home, and go to bed.

Once a month, Moira goes into the city with her grandmother. She loves seeing all the traffic, the people, and the tall buildings. They ride a taxi past Third, Fourth, and Fifth Avenues. Then they stop at a large department store. Moira's grandmother wants to buy a dress, a pair of shoes, and a purse. Moira soon gets tired. She can't wait to get back in the car, drive home, and go to bed.

Name ______________________ Date __________

BLM 2 Grammar (Compound Sentences)

Read the story and underline the compound sentences. Then write each compound sentence on the lines below.

The Statue of Liberty stands 152 feet high, and it weighs 225 tons. Many people see her, and they can't believe her size. She carries a torch in her right hand, and she holds a tablet in her left. She was a gift from the French government. Years ago, the French and Americans placed her in New York Harbor.

Compound Sentences

The Statue of Liberty stands 152 feet high,

and it weighs 225 tons.

Many people see her, and they can't believe her size.

She carries a torch in her right hand, and

she holds a tablet in her left.

Name ______________________ Date __________

BLM 2 Grammar (Subject-Verb Agreement)

Read the story and circle the incorrect verbs. Write the correct verb above each circle. Then write the story correctly on the lines below.

My family and I walks [walk] a long way to California. The days and weeks on the trail is [are] long and hard. Sometimes it are [is] very dry. We chokes [choke] and coughs [cough] on the clouds of dust. It rain [rains] and snow [snows] on our trip. Then the road are [is] muddy. At times, the horses could hardly walk.

My family and I walk a long walk to California. The days and weeks on the trail are long and hard. Sometimes it is very dry. We choke and cough on the clouds of dust. It rains and snows on our trip. Then the road is muddy. At times, the horses could hardly walk.

Name ______________________ Date __________

BLM 2 Grammar (Abbreviations)

Read the story and circle the incorrect abbreviations. Write the correct abbreviation above each circle. Then write the story correctly on the lines below.

Last week, I went to see my doctor on Clark Sts. [St.] Drr. [Dr.] Carter couldn't believe how tall I was. Neither could his nurse, Msr. [Mrs.] King. The chart said that in Octo. [Oct.] I was 49 inches tall. In Feb [Feb.] I was 52 inches tall. Now I am taller than all the kids on Baker Ave.

Last week, I went to see my doctor on Clark St. Dr. Carter couldn't believe how tall I was. Neither could his nurse, Mrs. King. The chart said that in Oct. I was 49 inches tall. In Feb. I was 52 inches tall. Now I am taller than all the kids on Baker Ave.

Name ______________________ Date __________

BLM 2 Grammar (Possessive Nouns)

Read the story and circle the incorrect possessive nouns. Write the correct word above each circle. Then write the story correctly on the lines below.

Uncle Wills [Will's] airplane is really small. It is like flying around in the Reeds [Reeds'] van. Flying in his plane made my only brothers [brother's] stomach feel sick. But I do not mind the bumps, and I think the planes' [plane's] seats are cozy. I like to look down at people's houses. It is fun to wonder about each families' [family's] life.

Uncle Will's airplane is really small. It is like flying around in the Reeds' van. Flying in his plane made my only brother's stomach feel sick. But I do not mind the bumps, and I think the plane's seats are cozy. I like to look down at people's houses. It is fun to wonder about each family's life.

Name ______________________ Date __________

BLM 2 Grammar (Letters: Form and Punctuation)

Read the letter and circle incorrect or missing capitalization and punctuation. Write the correct capitalization or punctuation above each circle. Then write the letter correctly on the lines below.

may 12 2001

dear aunt Anne

Thank you for the interesting book. You always know the best books to read? It was fun learning about the life of a skater. Now I want to practice even harder

sincerely!

Grace

May 12, 2001

Dear Aunt Anne,

Thank you for the interesting book. You always know the best books to read. It was fun learning about the life of a skater. Now I want to practice even harder.

Sincerely,

Grace

74 Unit 6 Lesson 8 Intervention Blackline Masters

Name ______________________ Date __________

Comprehension Assessment

1. This story is mostly about
   - ● a boy who gets a bike
   - ○ a boy and his mother
   - ○ riding a bike
2. Which of these is most important to Alan's mother?
   - ○ riding very far
   - ○ riding fast
   - ● riding safely
3. Where will Alan ride first?
   - ○ to his friend's house
   - ● to his cousin's house
   - ○ to school with a friend
4. Before he started riding, what did Alan do first?
   - ○ looked at his tires
   - ○ waved to his mother
   - ● put on his helmet
5. When Alan gets to his cousin's house, he will
   - ● call home
   - ○ ride some more
   - ○ eat a snack

Name ______________________ Date __________

Vocabulary Assessment

Read the sentences. Draw a line under each compound word.

1. The cat saw something. It looked out the window. Then it ran through the doorway into the bedroom.

Read the sentences and look at the underlined word. Fill in the space beside the answer that means the opposite of the underlined word.

2. The floor of my room is very clean.
   ○ large ● dirty ○ flat
3. All the children were very quiet.
   ● loud ○ good ○ happy
4. I read a funny story last night.
   ○ long ○ strange ● sad

Read the sentences. Fill in the spaces beside the correct contraction that means the same thing as the underlined words.

5. This is not my coat.
   ○ isnt ○ is'nt ● isn't
6. Annie did not call me.
   ● didn't ○ did'nt ○ didnt
7. My friends are not ready yet.
   ○ arent ● aren't ○ are'nt
8. We will have a snack.
   ○ well ● we'll ○ w'ell

Name ______________________ Date __________

Skills Assessment

Read the sentences. Draw a line under each common noun. Draw a circle around each proper noun.

1. It was a warm day in July. The children swam in the cool water of Lake Waldo. Mary rowed her boat near the shore.

Read the sentences. Draw a line under each verb.

2. Kim walked quickly down the street. She saw her friend, Stan. He said hello to Kim. They talked for a little bit.

Read the sentences. Draw a line under the pronoun in each sentence. Draw a circle around the noun to which it refers.

3. Sam was tired because he had worked hard.
4. The house was small, but it was very nice.
5. Ask Linda and Chet if they want to play a board game.

Read the sentences. Draw a line under each adjective.

6. Put the new table beside the brown chair. We can put a small lamp on the table.

Read the sentences. Put the right punctuation mark at the end of each sentence.

7. That is a good story.
8. Did you eat lunch yet?
9. Watch out for that bee!
10. How old are you?

Name ______________________ Date __________

Comprehension Assessment

1. This story is mostly about children
   - ○ playing sports
   - ○ in school
   - ● helping
2. Which of these does Jenny do for Mrs. King?
   - ● mow the lawn
   - ○ read a book
   - ○ wash a car
3. After they raked leaves, Brad and Jenny
   - ○ went swimming
   - ● had a snack
   - ○ watched a video
4. A good title for this story is
   - ○ "A Job"
   - ○ "Playing"
   - ● "Helping"
5. Who does Mrs. King know?
   - ○ Jenny's mother
   - ● Brad's grandmother
   - ○ the teacher in school

Name ______________________ Date __________

Vocabulary Assessment

Read the sentences. Fill in the space beside the adjective that fits best in the blank.

1. Who caught the __________ fish, you, Tom, or Donna?
   ○ big ● biggest ○ bigger
2. It is __________ today than yesterday.
   ● colder ○ cold ○ coldest
3. We stopped playing because it was __________.
   ○ darkest ○ darker ● dark

Read the sentences. Draw a line under each time or order word.

4. The first thing the campers did was put the tent up. Then they started a fire. After that, they cooked their supper. Finally, they went to sleep.

Read the sentences. In the blank, write the plural form of the word in parentheses.

5. There were too many (fly) ___flies___ at the picnic.
6. My dog had five (puppy) ___puppies___.
7. The tree had more (cherry) ___cherries___ than last year.

Read the sentences. Fill in the space beside the word that means the same as the underlined word.

8. The duck swam below the water.
   ○ around ○ above ● under
9. A loud noise made us jump.
   ● sound ○ light ○ song
10. Don't trip on that big rock.
   ○ log ● stone ○ rope

Name ______________________ Date __________

Skills Assessment

Read the sentences. Fill in the space beside the verb that is spelled right and fits in the blank.

1. The phone __________ a few minutes ago.
   ○ ring ● rang ○ ringed
2. Dad __________ his car keys, but found them.
   ● lost ○ lose ○ losed
3. Dana __________ the ball to Steve.
   ○ throwed ○ throw ● threw

Read the sentences. Draw a line under the pronoun in each sentence. Draw a circle around the noun to which it refers.

4. My sister hurt her knee playing soccer.
5. Laura and Matt want Bud to call them.
6. Carol, can you help set the table?
7. The cat played with its ball.

Read the sentences. In the blank, write the possessive form of the word in parentheses.

8. One of the (car) ___car's___ tires is flat.
9. That is (Judy) ___Judy's___ pen.
10. My uncle showed us an (owl) ___owl's___ nest.
11. This restaurant is (Chicago) ___Chicago's___ finest.
12. Give me all the (boys) ___boys'___ hats.

Name ______________________ Date __________

Comprehension Assessment

1. A tiger and a zebra are alike because they both
   ○ are brown
   ● have stripes
   ○ like to hunt.
2. Where do tigers live?
   ● in India
   ○ in Africa
   ○ in America
3. A tiger is
   ○ easy to see
   ○ very small
   ● hard to see
4. Lions like to hunt
   ● zebras
   ○ tigers
   ○ fish
5. This story is mostly about
   ○ hunting
   ○ Africa
   ● animals

Name ______________________ Date __________

Vocabulary Assessment

Read the sentences. Fill in the space beside the word that fits best in the blank. Be sure to look at the words carefully and think about what they mean.

1. We will have a picnic at __________ school.
   ● our ○ are
2. Ellen will __________ juice for us.
   ○ by ● buy
3. We stopped playing because it was __________.
   ○ darkest ○ darker ● dark

Read the sentences. Fill in the space beside the word that fits best in the blank. Be sure to use the meaning of the sentence to choose your answer.

4. The water in the lake was __________. Which word means the water was not warm?
   ● cold ○ deep ○ clean
5. There were __________ clouds in the sky. Which word means there were lots of clouds in the sky?
   ○ few ○ no ● many

Read the question. Fill in the space beside the answer you think is best.

6. Fill in the space beside the word that has the prefix *un*.
   ○ under ● untie ○ until
7. Fill in the space beside the word that has the prefix *re*.
   ○ reach ○ ready ● refill
8. Fill in the space beside the word that has the prefix *dis*.
   ● dislike ○ dishes ○ distant

Name ______________________ Date __________

Skills Assessment

Write the plural form of each word

1. mouse ___mice___
2. house ___houses___
3. penny ___pennies___
4. beach ___beaches___

Read the sentences. Draw a line under each adjective. Draw a circle around each adverb.

5. The black cat jumped (quickly) onto the bed. It walked (carefully) to the soft pillow. The cat curled up in a tiny ball and took a nap.

Read the sentences. Fill in the circle beside the word that tells what kind of sentence it is. Put the right punctuation mark at the end of each sentence.

6. Look out for that ice!
   ○ statement ○ question ● shows strong feeling
7. How long did the game last?
   ○ statement ● question ○ shows strong feeling
8. The coat you are wearing is pretty.
   ● statement ○ question ○ shows strong feeling

Read the sentences. Fill in the space beside the sentence that has correct punctuation.

9. ● "What time is it?" asked Fred.
10. ○ Sue answered, It is about nine o'clock.

Read the sentences. Fill in the space beside the sentence in which the subject and verb are correct.

11. ○ Rabbits likes to eat carrots.
12. ● My friends ride their bikes after school.

Name ______________________ Date __________

Comprehension Assessment

1. What kind of museum was it?
   ○ art
   ● science
   ○ music
2. The skeleton was a
   ● dinosaur
   ○ elephant
   ○ whale
3. The last things the children saw were
   ○ plants
   ○ bones
   ● eggs
4. Who was always asking questions?
   ● Wally
   ○ Nick
   ○ Carol
5. Another word for really big is
   ○ pretty
   ● huge
   ○ about

Name ______________________ Date __________

Vocabulary Assessment

Read the sentences. Draw a circle around the compound word in each sentence. A compound word is made up of two smaller words.

1. The family took a vacation on a (houseboat).
2. Bev's father went to sleep in the (armchair).
3. At the end of the trail was a beautiful (waterfall).

Read the sentences. In the blank, write the correct form of the adjective in parentheses.

4. The kitchen is the (warm) ___warmest___ spot in our house.
5. The lawn is (green) ___greener___ this year than last year.
6. The lion in the zoo was (loud) ___louder___ than the tiger.
7. The third problem was the (easy) ___easiest___ on the test.

Read the words. Draw a circle around the word in which only the root word is underlined.

8. (replay) replay replay
9. deepest (deepest) deepest
10. reading reading (reading)

Name ______________________ Date __________

Skills Assessment

Read the sentences. Fill in the space beside the sentence that has correct punctuation.

1. ○ Prizes will be given for first, second and, third place.
2. ○ The new store sells bikes skis and snowboards.
3. ● Our library has books, magazines, and newspapers.

Read the sentences. Fill in the space beside the answer that tells if it has a compound subject or compound predicate.

4. Mary and Cathy joined the swimming team.
   ● compound subject ○ compound predicate
5. Gina rose and walked to the front of the room.
   ○ compound subject ● compound predicate
6. The bus turned the corner and stopped near the school.
   ○ compound subject ● compound predicate
7. Ice and snow fell from the roof onto the sidewalk.
   ● compound subject ○ compound predicate

Read the sentences. In the blank, write the correct abbreviation for the word in parentheses.

8. My aunt lives on Market (street) ___St.___.
9. The children visited (mister) ___Mr.___ Stanley.
10. (Doctor) ___Dr.___ Smith lives here.
11. Kendra walked down Fifth (Avenue) ___Ave.___.
12. Our school is on Willow (Road) ___Rd.___.

Name ________________________ Date __________

Comprehension Assessment

1. This story is most like
   - ● a real story
   - ○ a fairy tale
   - ○ a poem

2. Why does Ollie's tummy feel funny?
   - ○ He ran home from school too fast.
   - ○ He ate too much.
   - ● He knows he did something wrong.

3. The mistake Ollie made was
   - ○ giving flowers to his teacher
   - ● not asking Mr. Lake
   - ○ leaving school early

4. Ollie's parents are proud because he
   - ○ always does his homework
   - ○ knows that people like flowers
   - ● told Mr. Lake he was sorry

5. If someone has courage, they are
   - ○ foolish
   - ● brave
   - ○ careful

Name ________________________ Date __________

Vocabulary Assessment

Read the sentences. Fill in the space beside the word that means the same as the underlined word.

1. The <u>boat</u> sailed across the lake.
   ○ box ○ raft ● ship
2. Jeff carried a <u>sack</u> of groceries.
   ○ box ● bag ○ basket
3. The tiger <u>dashed</u> into the jungle.
   ● ran ○ jumped ○ crawled

Read the sentences. Fill in the space beside the word that fits best in both sentences.

4. The plane will __________ soon.
   The farmer grew corn on her __________.
   ○ arrive ● land ○ farm
5. Did you put your money in the __________?
   Trees grew on the __________ of the stream.
   ● bank ○ wallet ○ side

Read the question. Fill in the space beside the answer that means the opposite of the underlined word.

6. George <u>filled</u> the bottle with water.
   ● emptied ○ poured ○ washed
7. A <u>tiny</u> bird sat on the branch.
   ○ pretty ○ rare ● huge
8. The bed was too <u>soft</u> for me.
   ○ few ● hard ○ high

Name ________________________ Date __________

Skills Assessment

Read the sentences. Draw a line under each <u>position word</u>.

1. Brian swam <u>under</u> the boat. Sue looked <u>over</u> the side to see where he was. He surprised her by coming <u>up</u> quickly.

Read the sentences. Put <u>commas</u> in the right place in each sentence.

2. The park had many trees, shrubs, and bushes.
3. We will have a test in spelling, math, and science.
4. Leaves, sticks, and branches were all over after the storm.

Read the sentences. Draw a line under each <u>common noun</u>. Draw a circle around each <u>proper noun</u>.

5. On (Saturday) we will have a <u>party</u>. It is his <u>birthday</u>. We want to surprise him. His <u>parents</u> are giving him <u>skis</u>. They will go skiing in (December).

Read the sentences. Draw a line under each <u>adjective</u>. Draw a circle around each <u>adverb</u>.

6. A <u>long</u> pile of rocks went into the water. The waves crashed (loudly) against it. We walked (carefully) on the <u>slippery</u> stones.

Read the sentences. In the blank, write the <u>possessive form</u> of the word in parentheses.

7. A (bear) ___bear's___ claws can be three inches long.
8. A stone cracked our (car) ___car's___ windshield.

Read the letter. In the blank, write the correct form of the words in parentheses. Don't forget the punctuation marks.

9. (dear sammy) ___Dear Sammy,___
   I can't wait until we visit next week. Going fishing is one of the first things I want to do. I hope the weather is good.
10. (your cousin) ___Your cousin,___
Roberto

Name ________________________ Date __________

Comprehension Assessment

1. What did Nat probably do every day?
   - ○ go to school
   - ● write in his journal
   - ○ play sports with friends

2. From the story, you know that a schooner is a kind of
   - ● boat
   - ○ chair
   - ○ horse

3. When they reached Oregon, Nathaniel was
   - ○ upset
   - ● happy
   - ○ hungry

4. Which of these is true about the Oregon Trail?
   - ○ It was for boats.
   - ○ No one could find it.
   - ● Many people traveled on it.

5. People traveled in wagon trains mostly for
   - ● protection
   - ○ fun
   - ○ speed

Name ____________________ Date __________

Vocabulary Assessment

Read each sentence. Fill in the blank with the correct word from the homophones in parentheses.

1. A ranger (lead/led) __led__ the children through the park.
2. This metal is so heavy it must be (lead/led) __lead__ .
3. Last week, (our/hour) __our__ dog had puppies.
4. The movie will begin in one (our/hour) __hour__.
5. The answer to the problem is (ate/eight) __eight__ .
6. We (ate/eight) __ate__ pizza for dinner.

Read the sentences. Fill in the space beside the word that has the same root word as the underlined word in the sentence.

7. The Miller family has lived in our town more than 100 years.
   ○ glove ○ shovel ● alive
8. The handle of the cup is broken.
   ● handful ○ sandy ○ honest
9. The workers replaced the broken motor.
   ○ package ● placing ○ playful

Read the words. Fill in the space beside the compound word in each group.

10. ○ peaceful ○ vegetable ○ morning ● houseboat
11. ○ window ○ television ● daylight ○ elephant
12. ○ carried ● snowflake ○ dinner ○ package

Name ____________________ Date __________

Skills Assessment

Read the sentences. Fill in the space beside each answer that is a compound sentence.

1. ● The doorbell rang, and the dogs started barking.
2. ○ Movie stars and athletes are usually famous.
3. ● The pool is open, but it is too cold to swim.

Read the sentences. Fill in the space beside the sentence in which the subject and verb agree.

4. ○ A new store are coming to our town.
   ○ The children meets their parents at the bus stop.
   ● Hikers often climb the hill near our school.
5. ● Trains leave the station every hour.
   ○ A lion sleep after it eats.
   ○ A computer cost less than before.

Read the sentences. In the blank, write the correct past-tense form of the verb in parentheses.

6. My sister (catch) __caught__ a cold last week.
7. The worker (paint) __painted__ the house yesterday.
8. Some ducks (fly) __flew__ over the house earlier.

Read the sentences. Draw a line under each possessive noun that should have an apostrophe.

9. This books author is from our town.
10. Our class met our teachers father.